Leo Politi
Artist of the Angels

by Ann Stalcup

SILVER MOON PRESS

Edited by Hope L. Killcoyne
Layout and Design by Karin Lillebo

For information:
Silver Moon Press
New York, NY
(800) 874-3320

10 9 8 7 6 5 4 3 2 1

Library of Congress Cataloging-in-Publication Data

Stalcup, Ann, 1935-
    Leo Politi : artist of the angels / by Ann Stalcup.
       p. cm.
    ISBN 1-893110-38-9
    1. Politi, Leo, 1908---Juvenile literature. 2. Authors, American--20th
century--Biography--Juvenile literature. 3. Artists--United States--Biography--Juvenile
literature. 4. Children's stories--Authorship--Juvenile literature. 5. Illustration of
books--Juvenile literature. I. Politi, Leo, 1908- II. Title.

PS3531.O255Z89 2004
813`.54--dc22
[B]
                                                    2004056568

Song of the Swallows artwork on the cover and on pages 37 and 39 is reprinted with
the permission of Atheneum Books for Young Readers, an imprint of Simon and
Schuster Children's Publishing Division. [Song of the Swallows by Leo Politi, copyright
1948 Charles Scribner's Sons; copyright renewed (c) 1976 Leo Politi.]

This book is dedicated to my husband, Ed, with grateful thanks for his support and for his interest in this project, for accompanying me on interviews, and for his endless patience in reading and re-reading my manuscript.

To Lyn Apodaca, my dear friend, for introducing me to Leo and for sharing with me her passion for his work. Unfortunately, she didn't live to see the completion of this book.

To Paul Politi and Suzanne Bischof, Leo's son and daughter, for their cooperation, for their enthusiasm for this project, and for their wonderful stories of Leo.

And to my editor, Hope Killcoyne, who made my book "sing" through her skillful questions, comments, and additions.

I would like to acknowledge the following people who so generously shared their memories of Leo: Richard Alonzo, Carlos Callejo, Debbie Conti, Thom Davis, Keri Dearborn, Mike Dreebin, Sid Fleischman, Gim Fong, Sol Grossman, Bill Chun Hoon, Mary Yan Joe, Tony Johnston, Harvey D. Kern, Peggy Miller, Norman Niccoll, Carmen Santana, Sandy Schuckett, Don Allen Shorts, Catherine Siracusa, Bill Sousa, Alice Sousa-Madrid, Carolyn Tokunaga, and Kathleen Turgeon.

Thank you to the following publications for their permission to include article excerpts:
LOS ANGELES DOWNTOWN NEWS: "Hill's Angel" by Rob Kendt
THE HORN BOOK: "Leo Politi: Friend of All" by Rosemary Livesey
THE LOS ANGELES TIMES: Columns by Jack Smith
THE REDLANDS DAILY FACTS: "Politi Wanted a Relaxing Landscape" by Nelda Stuck
THE REDLANDS SUN: "A Sentimental Look at Redlands" by Rosemary Hite
THE TIDINGS: "Politi Looks at the City He Loves" by Rich Goul; "The Gift for Los Angeles," no author listed
CATHOLIC AUTHORS, Volume 2, St. Mary's Abbey, 1952: "Leo Politi," Matthew Hoehn, editor

The photograph on page *vii* appears by permission of the *Fresno Bee*. The photograph on page 18 appears by permission of the Security Pacific Collection/Los Angeles Public Library. The lyrics to "Nature Boy," by Eden Ahbez, on page 93, appear by permission of Warner Bros. Publications U.S. Inc. The illustrated map on page 24 was created by Michael Collins.

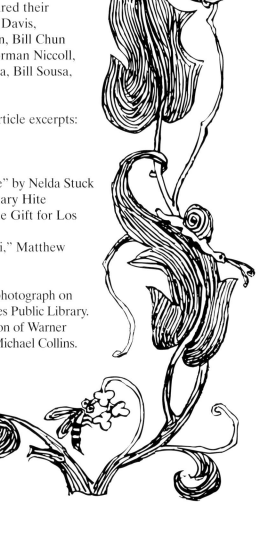

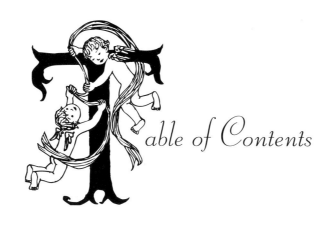

Table of Contents

Foreword

This studio photo of Leo Politi was taken in the 1940s. It appeared on the back flap of *The Mission Bell*.

Although Leo Politi has many loyal fans—especially in his native California—many of you may not have heard of him. Some of you, or perhaps your parents or grandparents, may have read his most famous book, *Song of the Swallows*. It tells of the miraculous 7500-mile journey of tiny birds that fly from Goya, Argentina, to a small church court-yard in California every year, then back again. If the title doesn't ring a bell, the cover art, with its gold Caldecott Medal sticker, probably does. Over the course of five decades, Leo wrote many, many more books. But fame, unlike swallows, does not necessarily alight at the same spot year after year. Nonetheless, for anyone who ever read Leo's stories, or was lucky enough to meet the smiling, owl-eyed man with the well-used drawing board and fast-moving pencil, his memory is warm, colorful, and lasting.

Leo's early childhood was the stuff of storybooks. Until he was six, Leo lived on a California ranch with his parents and sister, Marie Therese. Each day must have seemed like a holiday as the two children rode the family's Shetland ponies and played games in the endless California sunshine. Then Leo's parents decided to move back to Italy. Perhaps they thought a better living could be earned there. Unfortunately, money never poured in, but family troubles did. Leo's parents separated, and Leo was raised apart from Marie Therese. Even so, he found comfort and happiness in looking at the larger world around him and bringing it down to sketchbook size. Leo drew everything—the arch of an old building, green leaves pointing toward the sky, a dog in the sun.

As he grew through adolescence and adulthood—right up to his final, eighty-seventh year, Leo, the artist, writer, and observer, retained a purity and innocence that passing years usually erase. His son, Paul, describes him as "childlike but not childish." Leo never cared about money. His love of history, nature, and children motivated everything that he did, inspiring his paintings, drawings, and the stories he told. His books brim with harmony, happiness, and the true wealth found in relationships. In his lifetime, Leo wrote and illustrat-ed twenty-four books, illustrat-ing nearly twenty more for other authors. Throughout, he created stories and images that speak to the child in all of us.

It all started long ago in central California, back in the days when messages were delivered by trained pigeons and mail was trotted along by horse-drawn carriages . . .

Somewhere between the Civil War-era mail deliveries of Pony Express and the overnight service available today, Fresnans received their letters via horse-drawn vehicles such as this one.

Reprinted by permission of *The Fresno Bee*

Chapter 1
The Indian Suit

Atiglio Leoni Politi, better known as Leo Politi, was born on a sunny Saturday in Fresno, California, on November 21, 1908. He was the second child of Italian immigrant parents, Lodovico and Mary Politi. Two years earlier, in 1906, Leo's parents and grandparents (Lodovico's mother and father) had moved from Italy to America. It was the turn of the century, and people from all over Europe were leaving the old world for the new one, trying to make a better life for themselves. Most immigrants, the Politis included, first set foot on U.S. soil at Ellis Island, New York City. Although remaining in the city long enough for the birth of their first child—Leo's big sister Marie Therese—the Politis did not make New York their home. They were country folk from a small village in northern Italy who wanted surroundings that felt familiar. Determined to find the right place, the family continued westward. It wasn't until they reached California that they found their dream. In the fertile farmlands surrounding Fresno, they finally arrived at the place to start a new life. Leo's grandparents bought a vineyard. His parents bought a small ranch. Fresno seemed to be the answer to the family's prayers.

Baby Leo, his sister, Marie Therese, and their parents, Lodovico and Mary Politi, posed for this photograph in Fresno, California, in 1909.

Little Leo lived with his father and mother and sister in a ranch house in California. Leo's father and mother had come to America from Italy. (Little Leo)

Lodovico was a friendly man. He loved to laugh and sing, and he made friends easily. Mary was more reserved, but she was a loving woman, always quick to help those who were in trouble. She was interested in all types of fine arts and wrote poetry in her spare time.

But there wasn't much spare time. Even on a small ranch, life was busy. There were chickens and horses to feed, eggs to collect, water to pump, and repairs to be made to the buildings and equipment. For Leo's parents, there was little time for anything else.

Leo and his sister were happy to keep themselves entertained. They loved the freedom of country life, spending many hours riding the family's Shetland ponies. The ponies were just the right size for two small children. They always rode bareback.

Leo and his sister loved riding the ponies. Leo would ride in front, Marie in back. *(Little Leo)*

Often business took Leo's father into nearby Fresno. Lodovico earned a living by buying and selling horses. He even sold horses to Buffalo Bill for his Wild West Show. Buffalo Bill, whose real name was William Cody, was one of the most colorful figures in the Old West. His show used actual cowboys and Indians, and made him world famous. He used his fame to fight for conservation, as well as the rights of Indians and women. That Buffalo Bill bought some of Lodovico's horses meant that they were really fine horses.

When Lodovico returned from a business trip he sometimes brought back gifts for Leo and Marie. On one occasion, when Leo was six years old, Lodovico brought something for everyone. For his wife, Mary, there was a big hat trimmed with roses. Little Marie received a beautiful blue bonnet. And Leo was given the gift he wanted most of all—an Indian chief's suit.

From then on, Leo wore his Indian suit every day. Letting out loud war cries, he made the chickens squawk and flap their wings and run away. The dog barked and the horses pricked up their ears nervously as Leo raced around the farmyard. Sometimes Leo performed rain dances, or crawled on his belly as he had seen Indians do in movies. In his mind, he was an Indian.

But the fun ended one day when Papa announced that he was moving the family back to Italy. In what seemed like no time at all they were on their way. After selling their farm for only a few hundred dollars, the Politis packed up their belongings and began the long journey back to Italy. Leo felt very unhappy when Papa sold their beloved horses and ponies. Leo asked the man who bought them to promise to take good care of them. The man promised that he would.

There was sadness, but for the two children it was also the beginning of an exciting adventure. They would travel by train and boat and see many new places. The journey would take several weeks. When Leo asked if he could wear his Indian suit the entire trip, his mama told him that he could. Once again, the Politis traveled across America, this time heading east. Leo left Fresno wearing his Indian suit, Marie her beautiful blue bonnet.

Chapter 2
Farewell to Fresno

The Politis traveled across the United States by transcontinental train. The scenery changed many times as they covered mile after mile and state after state. They saw mountains and deserts, plains and fertile farmland. They crossed rivers and passed through small towns and large cities. Often Leo and Marie rode on the outside platform at the end of the train. They wanted to make sure that they didn't miss a thing. It was quite an adventure for two young children.

Leo couldn't believe what an exciting city New York was. He had never seen buildings so tall! Noisy trains ran above and below the street. It was so different from the peace and quiet of the ranch in California. Everyone they passed seemed to be staring at them. *Was it his Indian suit*, Leo wondered? *Marie's blue bonnet?*

The Politis crossed the Atlantic by ocean liner, the only way you could make the journey in those days. Mama was very seasick, but the two children had a wonderful time. There were so many places to hide and explore. The captain took Leo onto the bridge of the ship and showed him how to steer. He showed Leo how to use binoculars to see what was ahead. Leo showed the

RIGHT: *The Captain took Leo on the bridge to show him how to steer the ship. Leo liked this best of all. (Little Leo)*

captain how Indians shade their eyes with their hands when they want to see a long way, and the captain copied him.

When the boat finally docked in Italy, the journey was still not over. Papa hired a man with a horse and buggy to take them the rest of the way. They were going to northern Italy, to the top of Italy's "boot." Just south of Milan lay Broni, the hillside village

where Mama's parents lived. Mama no longer felt sick. She excitedly pointed out vineyards and oxcarts as they bumped and bounced along the rough, unpaved road. Leo and Marie were seeing their mother's beloved Italy for the first time.

When the Politis reached Broni everyone came out of their homes to see the American newcomers. It was not often that strangers came to the village. The children were especially curious about Leo's costume. There was no movie theater in the town, nor one nearby, so they had no idea why Leo was dressed as he was, or even what an Indian was.

Mary's parents were overjoyed to see the children. As both Leo and Marie had been born in America, it was the first time the grandparents had met their grandchildren. A large pot of ravioli simmered in the fireplace, there was cool water from the well, and fresh bread baked in the outdoor oven. The village children peered through the kitchen window to see what was going on. As the family ate their meal, there was a great deal of laughter as everyone tried to talk at once. There was so much news to exchange! Leo's grandparents' home brimmed with joy.

But beyond their home, village, and country, trouble was brewing. The year was 1914. Within months, a war would rage throughout Europe. It was both an uncertain time and place to start a new life.

Chapter 3
Il Piccolo Americano

World War I swept across Europe, but luckily Broni remained much the same quaint, sleepy hill town it had been when Leo's mother had lived there as a child. Little by little, the Politi family settled into village life. Leo's father worked hard to support the family. He tried many kinds of jobs, including buying a restaurant and selling horses as he had done in California. It was a struggle.

For Leo, though, adapting to life in Italy was easy. His family had always spoken both Italian and English. Since he already knew Italian, it didn't take long for him to make friends at school. Wearing his Indian suit every day, he quickly became a classroom sensation. His Italian classmates had never seen an Indian before, and Leo told them many stories about the cowboys and Indians he had seen in movies at home in America. And of course, he made the stories more and more exciting each time he told them!

Although the students were impressed with Leo's fringed shirt and pants, the bright-feathered headdress hanging down his back was what they admired most. They called Leo *il piccolo Americano*, the little American, and followed him wherever he went. In school, he became such a distraction that the teacher asked that he not wear the suit again. After that, Leo only wore his costume when the school day was over.

The children of Broni wished that they had suits and head-dresses like Leo's, so Leo came up with a plan. He told the children to ask their mothers for any old cloth they could find. They were also to find as many chicken feathers as they could. It wasn't long before all the mothers and children in the village were busy making Indian outfits. The children painted the feathers the brightest colors they could find while the mothers cut and stitched scraps of fabric. Before long, the village was full of Indians! The children ran and played everywhere, whooping with loud war cries wherever they went, just as Leo had seen the Indians in the movies do. It was most certainly a Hollywood version of Native Americans, but the children of Broni, Italy—Leo included— thought they were quite convincing. "Wa-wa-wa-wa-wah" was heard from dawn to dusk in the village. In a long line behind Leo, the children ran across the town square, up and down the hills, and through the narrow streets. The small village was no longer peaceful, but the people who lived there were happy to see the children having such a good time.

But all was not well in the Politi household. Crossing a continent and an ocean did little to solve Mary and Lodovico's problems after all. Unfortunately, soon after arriving in Italy, Leo's parents separated. Although both Lodovico and Mary were constant in their support of Leo and his sister, at times brother and sister lived apart. Money, too, remained a family problem. But not for Leo. Though money was scarce, he managed to have fun,

RIGHT: *They followed him everywhere he went. They followed him to school and followed him home. They could not keep their minds on their lessons. (Little Leo)*

especially at Christmas. Although the only gift he received was a sock with an orange and a few nuts inside, to Leo it was a very special, memorable gift.

Somehow, by 1920, the family had managed to scrape together enough money for a special yearlong trip to London, England. Adaptable as ever, Leo didn't find the students and teachers at his new school much different from those he had known in Italy. He attended one of London's parochial (church) schools where the students and neighboring community were Italian.

After school, however, Leo's life was quite different from what he had known. Clearly, London was no isolated, sleepy hillside village, nor a sunny California horse ranch. City life may not have been what he was used to, but for Leo, it was thrilling. Twelve years old, he was allowed the freedom to explore this strange and wonderful world on his own. A budding artist, Leo wanted to visit the museums and gaze at the great masters' work. Although he would be greatly influenced by the artists represented there—among them Edgar Degas, Vincent van Gogh, and Auguste Renoir—he was just as impressed by what was outside the museums, beneath his feet: chalk drawings. Leo became enthralled by the sidewalk artists who so swiftly and skillfully created works of art using only chalk as their medium, sidewalks as their canvas. If you've ever seen the movie *Mary Poppins*, you may remember Bert the chimney sweep as having been a talented, even magical, chalk artist.

Before long, Leo's nose led him to another London treat: fish and chips. After one bite, Leo was hooked. Sprinkled with malt vinegar and salt and served in newspaper cones, fish and chips (French fries) made a delicious and cheap meal for the young artist. In one form or another, a love of sidewalk meals and sidewalk art would stay with Leo throughout his life.

When Leo turned thirteen, the family returned to Italy. Once again in Broni, Leo easily slipped back into the slower pace of Italian village life. With the inspiration of a year in England fresh in his mind, he looked around Broni with a new artistic eye. Using any scraps of paper he could find, Leo spent countless hours drawing and painting everything he saw. He was also fascinated with puppets and the work of puppeteers. Perhaps that interest was kindled back when he first came to Italy and had come across what would become his favorite book, *Pinocchio*. Of course, Leo wasn't the only one who loved the story—it was Italy's number one book for children—but he was so particularly enthralled by the tale of the little puppet who becomes a boy that he wanted to become a puppeteer himself, or at least some kind of artist. He wasn't sure which. But Leo did know that with each painting, sketch, and wood carving, he would make art his life. With great certainty, the thirteen-year-old announced his intentions to his mother and father.

An artist? A puppeteer? Some parents might have objected. Although the Politis were poor, and they thought it was unlikely that he would ever make much money as an artist, Mary and Lodovico encouraged and nurtured Leo's dream. It was what he wanted, and his talent was evident.

Mary lost no time lending helpful support to her son's dream. She learned of a competition for a scholarship to the National Art Institute. Teenagers from all over Italy were eligible. Mary persuaded Leo to enter. At age fourteen, he was chosen as the winner from all of northern Italy. There at the famous and beautiful art school in the Royal Palace at Monza, not too far from Milan, Leo lived the life of an artist.

In addition to painting and drawing, he studied sculpture, architecture, and design. His teachers showed him new ways to improve his artistic skills by focusing on his surroundings—not just what he observed with his eyes, but what he felt of the life force within. One particularly inspirational teacher, Ugo Zovetti, made a lasting impression on the young artist. Leo later recalled, "He would take a small flower and gently open it to show us its beautiful lines, shapes, and colors. When we were drawing birds and animals he taught us not to see them as static objects but to seek the inner life . . ."

Every day Leo made his way about the lush grounds and nearby parks, watching and drawing birds, people, and flowers, feeling their inner energy and light. Sketching from life became Leo's passion, one that would remain with him forever.

This painting, created by Leo when he was a teenager, sat hidden for sixty years. Decades after the painting was done, Leo's son removed a photo from its frame and discovered this early work of his father's concealed underneath.

Leo's love of lush gardens and parks stayed with him throughout his life.

Beginning in art school and continuing throughout his career, Leo experimented with various styles and techniques. Just as you might use an expression you have heard, trying it on for size, artists and writers do a similar thing. Drawing or writing in the style of another—usually famous—creator is a good method of discovering new ways to express an image or thought.

But all was not scenery and sketchbooks. During Leo's six years at the Institute, he—along with all other able-bodied young men—was forced to spend some months in the Italian army. At that time, the mid 1920s, the Fascists, led by Italy's dictator, Benito

Mussolini, were in power. Mussolini had decreed that all young Italian men had to serve in the army. Of course, there wasn't a war going on, and so no real enemy to fight. It was a brief interruption to Leo's studies, an interruption he made the best of.

In 1928, Leo graduated from the Institute as a *Maestro d'Arte*. This qualification allowed him to teach art in Italy. But Leo knew that teaching was not how he wanted to spend his life. For a short while, he and a friend designed textiles (fabrics) and tapestries. They also did some scientific textbook illustrations. But neither was the kind of art that interested Leo.

What he really wanted to do was take his sketchbook and draw what he saw— for himself, and for any others who might enjoy seeing how he translated the world around them. A true independent spirit, Leo had no desire to follow the directions of those who might hire him. So in 1930, with sketchbooks and suitcases in hand, Leo said good-bye to his family and returned to the United States. To Leo, California was still home. And in California he thought he would have more opportunities to make a living as an artist.

Little did he know that it would be the journey as much as the destination that would profoundly affect his life, his work, and the way he would view the world.

Chapter 4
California, Here I Come!

Leo was twenty-one years old when he headed back to California. It was 1930. As he traveled by freighter through the Panama Canal and up along the Central American coast to reach Los Angeles, he fell in love with Mexico and the other countries of Central America.

Freighters make many stops along the way, giving their few passengers plenty of time to explore at each port as cargo is loaded or unloaded. As Leo stopped here and there, he became fascinated with the Latin American way of life. He was especially moved by the importance of family. From that time on, the people he met, the stories and songs he heard, and the culture and history he learned about worked their way from his heart to his art.

Although by now quite practiced at world travel, Leo found certain aspects of leaving behind one land for another still challenging. His main issue was food and drink. After months of being away from Italy, Leo had come to miss dearly his frequent cups of Italian espresso. He found that one of his hardest adjustments was getting through each day without that strong, rich, black coffee he had come to love in Italy. In the 1930s there were none of the many coffee houses that are so readily found today in the United States. And finding espresso? Impossible. To Leo, American-style coffee was pale, weak, and would not do. Food presented its own problems. Still missing the fish and chips of his London days, Leo resisted the Italian-American equivalent of a filling fast food: pizza. Like many Italians, he said it wasn't Italian!

Then there was the matter of finding a new home. Somewhat like Goldilocks, Leo tested this, that, and the other place before he found the one that was just right. Since he had relatives in Huntington Beach, he went there first. But he didn't stay long. From Huntington Beach Leo went back to Fresno where he had more relatives. There he met the woman he would marry, the beautiful Helen Fontes. Helen was working as a waitress in nearby Madera. While Leo was having a meal, he did a sketch of her. Apparently, she liked the sketch—and the artist.

But although Fresno had been his first, much-adored home, the adult Leo found it to be too rural. He liked the hum of city life, so he moved on to San Francisco. By this point Leo very much wanted to find a place to settle down, but San Francisco wasn't quite right for him, either. It was lovely, but almost too lovely. Leo wanted a place that was not quite so sophisticated. He also wanted a place with real Latin flavor. Looking back, he knew Fresno would not be where he lived, but it was where he had found love. Packing his bags once again, he returned there, to Helen. The two dated for a while and together finally found a place that suited both of them: downtown Los Angeles. In August 1934, Leo and Helen were married. They were poor, but in love, and finally, at home.

The early thirties was a time Leo described as "the gloom days of the Depression." Many Americans lost the money they had invested; others lost their jobs. It was not a good time to start a career in a new city and new country. To top it off, a career in art was probably the most difficult way of all in which to make a living.

Leo and Helen found a house to rent in Los Angeles, on Bunker Hill. Bunker Hill was a large, hilly area of steep, narrow streets and alleys that crowned the heart of the city. Victorian

TOP: Here is a 1940s photo of the Angels Flight funicular as seen from the bottom of Bunker Hill. A funicular is a single-track hillside railway with two passenger cars—one at the top and one at the bottom. As the brake is released on the upper car it starts a downward journey, its weight pulling the other car up the steep incline. A loop in the track halfway up allows the two cars to pass each other safely.

Reprinted by permission of the Los Angeles Public Library

LEFT: In *Piccolo's Prank*, organ-grinder Luigi and his pet monkey Piccolo perform for people in the park, then take the Angels Flight funicular railway to their home on the Hill.

Piccolo always looked forward to the cable car ride up Angels Flight. When the little trolley began to climb the steep hill, his eyes grew wide with wonder. The crowds on the street looked smaller and smaller. As the cable car climbed higher and higher, Luigi and Piccolo could see the whole city spread out before them. (Piccolo's Prank)

18

homes dotted the streets, studding the crown like so many jewels. Not far from the Politis' own hillside home was a picturesque funicular railway known as Angels Flight. For a nickel, you could ride from the bottom to the top of the Hill. Although Leo usually climbed the steep hill instead of riding up, the mini-railway fascinated him. He knew he would use it in his art someday.

Leo and Helen often went to the nearby Grand Central Market to buy fruit and vegetables. One day when they were exploring the area they went into the Old Plaza Church—Helen to pray and Leo to look around. When they came out they noticed Olvera Street less than a block away. Helen felt as if it was an answer to her prayer. For Leo, it was the answer to a quest. Here, all the warm memories of Central America came back to life. Leo had finally found the Latin spark he sought. For the rest of his life, much of what he learned about—and earned from—his art was inspired by Olvera Street and its people. This little street, the oldest in Los Angeles, was like a Mexican oasis, right in the center of the busy city.

In the early 1930s, Olvera Street was more alley than street. It had no *puestos* (stalls) down the center as it has now. But the old buildings, some of them dating from 1781 when the street was created, radiated history. Over time, Olvera Street gradually became even more picturesque than when the Politis had first seen it, but Leo liked it just as it was. "I thought I was in heaven to find this street." Then as now, cars were off-limits; it was for pedestrians only. Artists, craftspeople, and merchants, most of them from Mexico, gave the street color and sound. Candle makers, glassblowers, silversmiths, furniture makers, and blacksmiths all were hard at work. The rich and tangy smells of Mexican food wafted through the air. On their first visit, Leo and Helen were two among many taking in the scenery, for as always, tourists, movie people, and locals filled the street.

In those days, Olvera Street was like New York City's Greenwich Village, or artsy sections of Paris, France. Leo described it as "a concentration of all the creative talents—motion picture movie stars, directors, producers, writers, puppeteers, artists . . . they all came there at night." Thanks to the efforts of a local socialite, Christine Sterling, the once-dilapidated buildings were spruced up and restored, trees were planted, and a pocket of the city was spared the usual urban "progress."

For the many Mexican families in Los Angeles, Olvera Street was a place to enjoy the sights, sounds, and smells of their homeland. It was also a place where parades and special celebrations were held. The Politis enjoyed the vibrancy, history, and sense of community. Raised in a farming family, Helen, whose parents were a mix of Portuguese and Spanish, felt right at home. During his years growing up in Broni, Milan, and London, Leo had been surrounded by historic old buildings and strong communities. Though Olvera Street was not Italian, Leo felt that he fit right in. It wasn't long before he began earning his living there.

In the 1930s there were outdoor tables in front of the street's El Paseo restaurant. Leo and several other artists were invited to set up their easels adjacent to the patio tables. At first Leo did charcoal portraits of tourists. Often, he had as much charcoal on his face and hands as he put down on the page! Although passersby would occasionally sit for a portrait, Leo barely made enough money to live on. But he never gave up hope.

Sometimes Leo and the other artists drifted to different restaurants to draw and paint. At other times they would set up their equipment in the plaza. When Leo tired of painting, he would whittle small wooden sculptures. For Leo and his artist friends, life was slow paced, sun filled, and pleasant. But to Mrs. Sterling, the woman responsible for saving Olvera Street, these artists sitting around were like nonpaying tenants. She thought it was high time for a change, and used her influence to make each and every one of them pay up. Leo, barely earning a living, was desperate. Luckily, the owner of El Paseo told him, "You can stay. You don't have to pay."

Leo and Helen showed up every day. Though the surroundings continued to be delightful, trying to keep Leo's would-be customers happy was often discouraging. Most people wanted portraits that looked just like them—or better. But neither direct imitation nor flattery was Leo's idea of art. So he put down the charcoal, picked up a brush and paint box, and began creating little scenes. "I spread them out on a table and sold them for ten cents apiece, twenty-five cents for three. Then I started creating characters from the children on the street and the dancers who entertained there. I started making bigger pictures." And people began paying Leo bigger prices—as much as fifty cents a drawing.

When work was slow, Leo enjoyed observing the work of other Olvera Street artists, particularly the puppeteers. Puppets were quite a big thing back then, and Leo had always been a fan. Famous puppeteers, including Edgar Bergen, a ventriloquist known for his puppet partner, Charlie McCarthy, also came to take in the Olvera Street scenery.

After hours of sketching, painting, woodcarving, and admiring other people's work, Leo's day often ended at midnight when he, Helen, and assorted artist friends walked up Temple Street to Leo's home on Grand Avenue. (In those days there were no freeways to cross.) As Leo later described it, "We'd sit on the street corner on the Hill [Bunker Hill]. The moon was above . . . we were all idealists. And we dreamed and talked about the world, and how it should be. There were a lot of wars then, and the Depression . . . but we had hopes all the time, and we had faith."

Leo also made friends, some of them lifelong friends, among the children he drew. One of them, Alice Sousa, was the daughter of a shop owner there. She noticed that Leo spent a lot of time observing people, and that it made him happy. Helen was usually with him. "Whenever we saw her," said Alice, "Helen wore a long black skirt, long-sleeved black turtleneck, black stockings, and shoes. Leo dressed in black, too. And he always wore a black beret on his head." Leo's beret made Alice and her friends think that he was French, since berets are traditional in France. It was quite a surprise when they found out much later that his background was Italian.

Bill Sousa, Alice's older brother, also came to know Leo well. Every day Bill rode the streetcar from school to his parents' store. Like many other children of local merchants, Bill grew up on Olvera Street and often spent time with Leo. The Depression was a financially desperate time for every family, but whenever Bill, Alice, or the other Olvera Street children came to watch Leo work, he gave them a dime or a nickel. In the 1930s, the movie theaters on nearby Broadway cost 15 cents; others cost a dime. It was a great treat for the children to receive Leo's gifts and be able to escape for a while into the world of movies. Leo loved children and was always generous towards them. Bill always remembered Leo's kindness.

Soon Leo became interested in Chinatown and Little Tokyo, also known as Japan Town. As time went by, he ventured to other parts of Los Angeles, as well, often sketching the colorful little houses of East Los Angeles or Chavez Ravine. With all his observations, sketches, and paintings of what he saw around him, Leo was not simply an artist but a "visual historian." Some years later, as the city grew and one district after another was forever changed, Chavez Ravine disappeared and Dodger Stadium was built on the site. Leo's many sketches preserve the past.

Leo truly loved his city, most especially its diversity. There were so many people living in downtown Los Angeles, people who had come from different parts of the world. He talked with the adults about their various customs and holidays, and enjoyed meeting and sketching the children, the "angels," of Los Angeles. In English, *los angeles* means "the angels."

Occasionally, Leo would venture out of the city, especially on smoggy days, which he hated. At those times, he would escape to parks or the beach. His favorite getaway was the Santa Monica Pier, another area that always hummed with life—and children.

But city or seaside, wherever Leo brought his easel, images of smiling children, soaring birds, and creeping vines swirled in his mind and onto the page. As the days, months, and years went by, words began mingling with the pictures. Watching the world around him, capturing it in dabs and lines, gestures and moods, Leo began to shape his stories.

RIGHT: Some of Leo's favorite places are noted in this map showing part of Los Angeles.

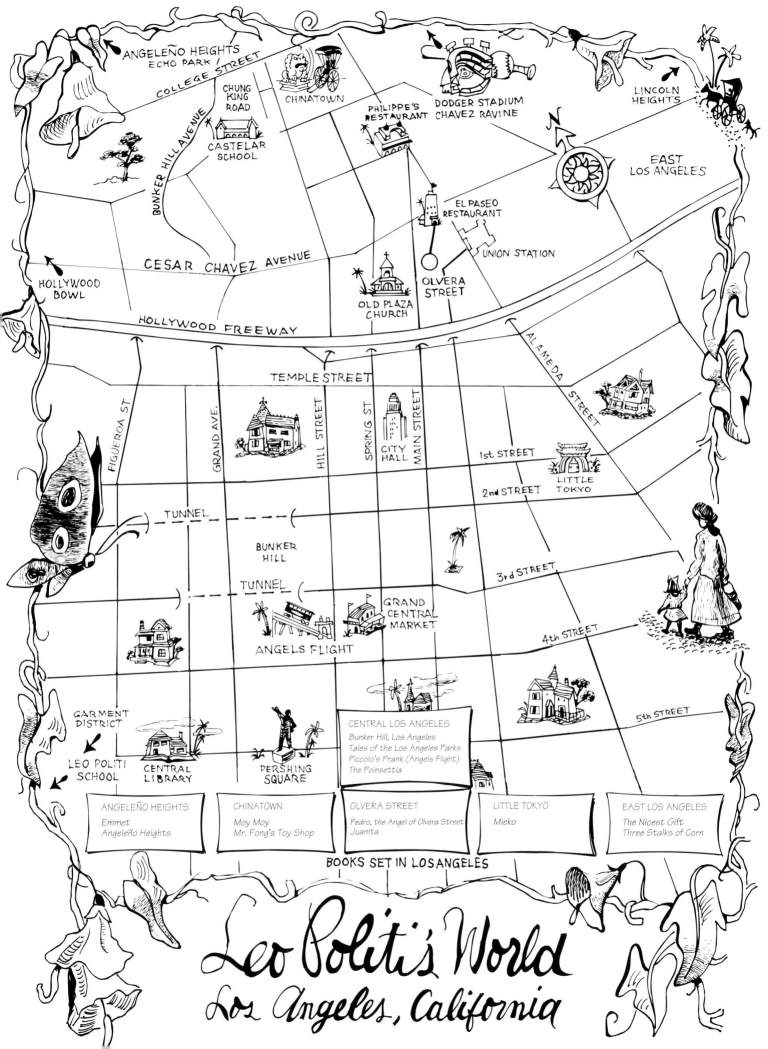

Chapter 5
Little Angels

     Beginning in 1938, several "little angels" came into Leo's life. Some arrived in the pages of his first books; two came into his and Helen's waiting arms. Paul Politi was born in 1943, his sister, Suzanne, in 1946.

     Leo's first "fictional" child was Little Pancho. As a character, Pancho was already known to Californians. He and other Mexican children, pictured doing all kinds of things from sewing to cooking to just hanging out, had graced the covers and pages of a sophisticated Los Angeles magazine, *Script*. *Script's* articles, drawings, and type made it look very much like the *New Yorker* magazine. *Script* often showcased important California writers. Leo, profiled in the May 25 issue in 1940, was proud of being a part of the same magazine that featured William Saroyan, whose writing he greatly admired. Another native son, Saroyan, too, was born in Fresno in 1908.

Pancho, Leo's mischievous little character, was actually based on a rather sad, heavyset child Leo had often observed on Olvera Street. The real little boy never smiled. Leo thought it might make

for a fun story to take the serious child and put him in an exotic, exciting world—the jungle of Central America. He then added two more Olvera Street characters to the mix: a young woman he noticed who always giggled and Coco, a local dog. Leo planned to take his "fictional child" and make him the star of a puppet theater production. But children—real or not—don't always follow the course their parents set for them, and in 1938, Pancho appeared not in a puppet play but in *Little Pancho*, Leo's first book.

Leo's cover for *Script* magazine shows Olvera Street in all its colorful hubbub. You can see the tiny shops (*puestos*), a musician, a red parrot, people selling ice cream and toys, and more. Can you find the sailors?

Leo's art style was quite different in *Little Pancho* from the artwork that appeared in his later books. As seen in these sketches, the paintings were caricatures rather than realistic portraits. *Little Pancho* was itself a little book, about the size of a CD case.

How did a sidewalk artist become an author/illustrator? Remember that Olvera Street was a popular destination for the many local movie people, some of them celebrities. Hollywood filmmaker Preston Sturges (the first Hollywood writer to direct his own script), strolling by one day, saw Leo's work displayed and bought every last drawing. Another movie person, New York City street kid turned actor John Garfield, became a close friend of Leo's. Many times the two would talk about the world and how to make it a better place. Not one to go to the movies himself, Leo did not learn that John was a famous actor for quite some time!

Leo actually had his own small brush with on-screen star-dom. Another of Leo's Olvera Street customers was a tall, imposing man, film director Fritz Lang. In Lang's 1945 classic *Scarlet Street*, Leo made an appearance as an extra for all of ten seconds. What was his part? A Greenwich Village sidewalk artist—not too much of a stretch! Leo enjoyed himself and was paid well. As he said, "A hundred dollars for about a minute . . . it was fun. I saw how they made movies."

One afternoon on Olvera Street, Leo spotted a pair of movie stars whom everyone back then recognized, even Leo: Clark Gable and Carole Lombard. Husband and wife, the handsome Hollywood legends were seated together at a table not too far from Leo's. Quickly, Leo sketched the actors, then happily brought over his drawings. As Leo chuckled years later about Gable's reaction to the sketches, "He didn't like them!"

Luckily, others did. Like calling "Electricity!" in a game of tag, where the one on base can extend a hand to a friend and make him safe, a chain of events and connections would soon electrify Leo's career. The chain began with an actress friend of Leo's who was a big fan of his work. She recommended Leo to her agent. The agent, in turn, was quite impressed with Leo's artistry, and arranged for him to have a one-man show of his art in New York City. The final link was a visitor to the show, May Massee, an editor at Viking Press, who became an instant Politi fan. Like a kid who makes it to base, Leo was "safe." May Massee was an influential editor. She liked Leo's Latin American-themed paintings and sketches, and thought his illustrations would be a good fit for some of Viking's upcoming books. Leo was very happy. But while one hand "touched base," he had something up his other sleeve: Pancho. He took the opportunity to send her the "dummy" book he had made. She liked that too! So it was that Leo's first fictional child was "born." His enthusiastic reaction? "Now I'm an author!"

With the publication of *Little Pancho*, Leo's life began to improve financially. He became a Viking Press artist, illustrating six books for them. He also created cover art for *Jack and Jill* (a children's magazine), sold political illustrations to newspapers, and continued to contribute covers and black-and-white sketches to *Script*.

But it was Leo's second book, *Pedro, the Angel of Olvera Street*, from which his long and fruitful career really took flight. That book not only had its origins in an Olvera Street contact, it was about Olvera Street itself. The idea grew out of handmade Christmas cards Leo had sent to several children's book editors he had come to know. The cards showed a little boy with red wings leading the street's annual Christmas celebration. Alice Dalgliesh, an editor at publisher Charles Scribner's Sons, was already a fan of Leo's work, having met him by chance one day while he was sketching on Olvera Street. Little did Leo know that meeting the vacationing editor from New York would change his life. Alice loved Leo's work and purchased some of his drawings and paintings. When he told her that he had a germ of an idea for a complete book based on the card, she was intrigued, thinking it would make a nice addition to the series she was editing about Christmas stories from other countries. She told Leo she would send an author to Los Angeles so that the two of them could work together. Leo was thrilled . . . at first. Then, as he recounted years later, he had second thoughts. "A week later I said to myself, 'I know this street, I know the children, I know everything there is to know. Why don't I try to write the story *myself*?'" He sent a letter to Alice, asking if he could make a little dummy book, words and all. She agreed. Liking what she saw, it wasn't long before *Pedro, the Angel of Olvera Street* was in bookstores and libraries across the country. For Leo's career, this was no mere game of tag. This was a major league home run.

Soon readers across the country discovered Leo's favorite place in the world, Olvera Street, as seen through Pedro's eyes:

He loved the little street because it was just as it was in the days of the past, with the red-tiled pavement and the old adobe houses—where the birds fluttered around the fountain and fed among the footsteps.

He loved the humble little *puestos* (shops) lined along the center of the street and bulging with colorful wares.

He loved the smells of good Mexican foods: tacos, tamales, enchiladas.

And music—there was always music everywhere.

And he loved Olvera Street because everyone was friendly and greeted him with a smile.

"Buenos dias, Pedro."

"Good morning, Pedro."

Pedro is set during *Las Posadas*, one of the most colorful of Olvera Street's special events. *Las Posadas* (*posada* is Spanish for shelter) is a Christmas procession that involves many Olvera Street shopkeepers and their children. It reenacts Mary and Joseph's arrival in Bethlehem and their search for shelter for the night. Shepherds and angels accompany Mary and Joseph on their search as they go from door to door, only to be turned away again and again.

For the nine nights from December 16 to December 24, Olvera Street holds its annual Las Posadas procession. Shopkeepers and their children carry candles as they reenact Mary and Joseph's search for a place to stay before Jesus was born. Pedro, with his red paper wings, leads the group. (Pedro, the Angel of Olvera Street)

One day Leo told Bill Sousa, one of the Olvera Street children, "You were one of the inspirations for my book *Pedro, the Angel of Olvera Street.*" Bill had always taken part in the annual Christmas and Easter parades on Olvera Street. It made him feel very proud to think that he might have inspired Leo's work.

The Politi family had a Christmas tradition of their own. Every December they strolled along, admiring the window displays in downtown Los Angeles department stores. Bullocks, Broadway, May Company, and Robinson's all had enchanting scenes on view, complete with animated figures and moving trains.

One of Paul's very favorite Christmases was when Robinson's used *Pedro, the Angel of Olvera Street* for its display. "Each window was a different page from the book," says Paul. "The words had been printed very large and each page was done with models. By the time you went to each window, you had read the whole book." The Politi children were completely delighted by what they saw. "It really touched me," said Paul. The family didn't own a camera so they don't have any pictures of it, but the memories remain just the same. "It made my dad even more special to me. I've never forgotten how proud I felt."

A few years after its publication Disney wanted to buy *Pedro* and make the story into an animated movie. Financial success was around the corner! Was Leo interested? Not at all. Money never interested him. He had strong ideas about the kind of work he would accept, and nothing would change his mind. He never took an assignment that made him uncomfortable. Tony Sousa, Bill and Alice's older brother, was one of the Olvera Street shopkeepers. Knowing how little money Leo earned and how much Disney would undoubtedly pay, he tried to persuade Leo to accept the deal, but Leo was adamant. He was sure Disney would change it and it would not be his book anymore. To Leo, art and integrity won over financial gain every time, no matter the circumstances. Years earlier, when money had been even tighter, he was offered an important commission for an advertising campaign by Union Oil. But Leo didn't like the assignment and wouldn't accept it. Helen had begged him to take it since it would have made a big difference in their lives financially, but she accepted Leo's decision when he turned down the job.

Most of Leo's time was still spent on Olvera Street, or in any other part of the city that interested him. He still sold sketches to tourists for as little as ten cents, and never more than $1.50. Those he did for himself he would transfer to canvas once he returned home. It would be around 10 o'clock at night before he started to paint, often continuing until almost dawn. It was up to Helen to keep Paul and Suzanne quiet until ten in the morning when Leo rose and his daily routine started again.

The hard work paid off when Leo's third book, *Juanita*, also set on Olvera Street, was published in 1948. The story centers on another Olvera Street tradition, the colorful Blessing of the Animals parade. On the Saturday preceding Easter Sunday, adults and children come from all over the city to have their pets blessed by a Catholic priest. Many Mexican families attend the parade in their traditional costumes. They and other visitors bring pets of all kinds and sizes: mice and mules, parrots and puppies, snakes and iguanas, any pet they wish to have blessed. In *Juanita*, Leo makes the parade come alive. If you ever visit Olvera Street on Easter Saturday, you, too, can take part in the annual parade.

Olvera Street is a place of parades and processions—at least a dozen festivities are scheduled there each year. The Blessing of the Animals parade, held every Easter Saturday, is the subject of *Juanita*. In this scene, families gather at the fountain before the parade.

Children came with all kinds of little animals and birds which looked so lovely with colored ribbons and wreaths of flowers. (Juanita)

34

Sometime in the late 1940s, Leo began making appearances at the nearby Los Angeles Central Library. He would meet with a group of children each week on the patio, who watched in awe as Leo drew. There, before their eyes, characters such as Pedro would appear on Leo's large sketch pad. He wanted them to know the joy and pride that come from creating. He showed them step

Leo loved to show how he drew his characters. Here he is in the late 1940s on the patio of the Los Angeles Central Library, enjoying one of his weekly how-to demonstrations.

by step how he made his characters and backgrounds, speaking of how he tried to feel the life within whatever he drew. Once, in 1949, when talking with the head children's librarian, Rosemary Livesey, Leo said, "I would like my children and all children to seek security less in material things, and more in the spiritual and the aesthetic; to know what it means to enjoy working with their hands; to be reasonable in what they want and generous in what they have to give."

Leo also began visiting schools. Though often uncomfortable and nervous when speaking to a group of adults, with children he felt completely at ease. On his visits he left behind at least one book for the school's library, always taking the time to paint a picture on the blank page at the beginning of every book. Usually he recreated one of the main characters in the book, but the illustration was not complete until he had written a loving message to the students.

Leo's school visits had a lasting impact on the children he met. Years later, writer Keri Dearborn vividly remembers the day he visited her school. She was seven or eight at the time. "Although Mr. Politi was thin and bent and his voice was high and cracked, he gave the impression of being a large man with a big aura . . . a man who was larger than life."

His one-on-one visits cast a spell, as well. Leo's friend, Sol Grossman, asked Leo to paint a portrait of Sol's then four-year-old granddaughter, about whom Sol himself said, "I must charitably describe [her] as hyper." But around Leo, she was anything but. Said Sol, "I sat in amazement as Leo kept her mesmerized during the two hours he worked on the painting. I have seen that same rapport with many other children since, and I am still amazed at his wonderful gift of communication with children . . . and adults as well."

Chapter 6
Song of the Swallows

Juan was full of curiosity about the swallows. He watched them build their small mud houses against the beams of the roof. (Song of the Swallows)

Leo not only enjoyed writing about Mexican culture and California life, he also found enjoyment writing about nature. It was a perfect fit, then, when his editor at Scribner's, Alice Dalgliesh, asked him to write a story about an annual California miracle. Her suggestion: write about the swallows that fly thousands of miles from Argentina to San Juan Capistrano and then back again every year.

On or about March 19, hundreds to thousands of cliff swallows fly to California's most famous mission, an old church and surrounding village founded by Spanish priests. Most of the birds leave again for their winter home on October 23. When Leo visited the lovely mission to do research for his story, he watched as the swallows swooped and twittered around the mission buildings. He was reminded of his childhood years in Italy when he had often watched swallows arcing through the sky. Picking up bits of mud here, grasses and feathers there, the birds built their nests under the roof beams of his grandparents' home.

At the mission, Leo was told about the old gardener, Julian, who had recently died. For many years, Julian faithfully rang the bell on March 19 to signal the return of the tiny travelers. Leo tucked away Julian as a potential character for his book. Now he needed a child. He didn't have to wait long. One afternoon, Leo noticed a young boy enthusiastically racing home from the mission to the little adobe house where he lived with his family. Ideas darted through Leo's mind like busy birds. Picking up bits of history here, details from nature there, a few Spanish words, and even a sense of spirituality, Leo soon built his most famous story.

"How wonderful the flight of the swallows is!" said Julian.

"Just try to picture, Juan, the hundreds and thousands of miles they travel, high up in the air, looking down over strange and beautiful lands.

I believe that, of all the creatures, God has given them the most freedom and happiness."

Song of the Swallows was published in 1949. When Leo won the Caldecott Medal for the book a year later, it was like a dream come true. The Caldecott Medal, awarded each year by the American Library Association, is the highest honor a children's book illustrator can win. The highest honor a children's book *author* can win is the Newbery Medal. Years later, in 1987, author Sid Fleischman, in his acceptance speech for *The Whipping Boy*, told the audience:

My turning from adult to children's books was the result of a chance remark. My daughter Jane came home waving a slip of paper that Leo Politi, on a visit to the children's room of the Santa Monica Public Library, had been kind enough to autograph. We crowded around to look at it, and my wife, quite innocently, remarked, "But you know, Daddy writes books, too."

It was Jane's answer that did it. "Yes," she said. "But no one reads his books."

Some people, like Sid Fleischman, are comfortable talking in front of groups. Other people are nervous. Leo was one of the nervous ones. When he traveled to New York to accept the Caldecott Medal, a cold settled in his back. Maybe it was nerves! But even with a backache, and even though he was, as always, jittery about speaking in public, nothing could mar his pleasure in the award he was about to accept.

LEFT: *Many birds came to the garden to nest, for here they were undisturbed . . . Julian always carried crumbs of hard bread in his pockets to feed them. The pigeons came and perched on his shoulders and on his hands. But the most joyous birds were the swallows. Juan called them by their lovely Spanish name, las golondrinas.* (Song of the Swallows)

When Leo gave his acceptance speech, many people learned for the first time the kind of man he was—his hopes and dreams; his interest in nature, ethnic customs, and traditions; and most of all his love of children. He may have been nervous, but he was eloquent. And modest:

> This honor, awarded to me for my *Song of the Swallows*, I should like to share with my editor, Miss Alice Dalgliesh. Without her encouragement and help, I doubt whether the other books I have written and illustrated for her—*Pedro, the Angel of Olvera Street* and *Juanita*, as well as *Song of the Swallows*—would ever have come into being.

He went on to talk about the process of design:

> I compose a book very much as if I were making a piece of sculpture. First I put down the bulk. When I feel the bulk has body and the right proportions, I begin to work on the detail. I work with the pictures and the text at the same time and make one supplement the other.

> In all my books I try to embody certain universal things—the warmth and happiness of family life; my love for people, animals, birds, and flowers. My love for the simple, warm and earthy things, from the humblest house to a little tree to the tiniest seashell; for the things made by hands, the sewing of a dress, the painting of a picture; and for the singing of songs and the movements of the body in dancing—all those arts which are instinctive forms of expression.

> I feel that it is only through the respect and continuity of our heritage that we can build a foundation with strong roots for our future.

After winning the Caldecott, Leo was frequently asked to speak at schools and libraries, something he still felt he could be better at. Determined to become more skilled and confident, he started going to Pershing Square in downtown Los Angeles to practice his oratory skills. In those days the park had a Speakers' Corner. Anyone who had something to say could stand on a wooden soapbox and speak, and crowds would gather around to listen. It took a lot of courage, but Leo stepped up on a box. He talked about politics or art or children—whatever was on his mind. It wasn't long before he became comfortable talking in front of large groups.

Confidence flowed through his written words and images, as well; Leo's work flourished. After *Song of the Swallows*, Leo wrote and illustrated *A Boat for Peppe*, set in an Italian American fishing community in Monterey, California. Soon after came *Little Leo*, Politi's autobiographic picture book. Next came *The Mission Bell*, the story of a huge bell that was brought from Spain to Mexico to California by dedicated priests, led, incidentally, by Father Junipero

The Mission Bell follows the journey of Spain's Father Junipero Serra and the soldiers and priests who accompanied him as they traveled from Mexico to California by mule and on foot. With them they carried a huge metal bell. It would hang in the first mission (church) Father Serra and his men built. In all, twenty-one missions were built along the California coast.

The big bell was removed from the oak tree and hung high up in the church tower, where it could be heard farther away. Its lovely sound rang out many times throughout the day; this and the happy voices of the people who sang as they went about their tasks filled the place with music and song.

Serra, who in 1776 had founded Mission San Juan Capistrano. Nature and history, art and words—all were coming together for Leo. Thanks to his editor, Alice Dalgliesh, Scribner's published all of these books—and many more. Scribner's always treated him like royalty, perhaps because of Alice's great admiration for his skill as an artist and storyteller.

An outing up the California coast to the Monterey Peninsula provided the material for his next book, *The Butterflies Come*. While he was there, Leo witnessed a miracle. High above the town of Pacific Grove, against the crisp blue sky, a broad swath of orange and black fluttered overhead. It was another wonder of nature—the monarch butterfly migration. In October, the monarchs arrive in a cloud. They stay peacefully in a grove of eucalyptus trees known locally as "Butterfly Trees." In spring they leave on their northward journey. Each year, their arrival is celebrated by a colorful, joyous parade as the children of Pacific Grove dance along the main street dressed as butterflies, caterpillars, or cocoons.

Inspiration sparked ideas. Leo imagined a boy, Stephen, and his younger sister, Lucia, as the central characters. The sketch pad was out, and Leo started writing:

> "Just think, Lucia, they come all the way from Canada, and they are such little things to travel so far. But the real mystery is—how they find their way back to a place they've never seen before. The old ones live only a few months—and everyone wonders what guides the young ones back to the butterfly trees."
>
> "If only the butterflies could talk, they could tell us," said Lucia.

RIGHT: *One day, as Stephen and Lucia were playing in the garden, they saw a strange cloud over the bay. As it came nearer they could see it was a cloud of thousands of orange butterflies glittering in the sunlight. As they passed overhead, Stephen and Lucia could hear the faint rustling sound of countless wings. (The Butterflies Come)*

Perhaps it's no wonder that journeys—natural or cultural—were so important to Leo. His own journeys—as a young child and a young man—had affected him quite deeply. As he matured into an author/illustrator, he worked this aspect of life into his life's work. From a relatively short procession down a city street to a 7500-mile journey across the sea, whether by human, animal, or both together, over half of Leo's books would highlight repeated journeys and how they give shape to life as they bring together the participants.

Chapter 7
Chinatown

When Leo wasn't sketching on Olvera Street, he could usually be found in Chinatown, a few blocks away. Reminiscing years later, Leo remembered going there on a cold night, eating Chinese food outside. "When I went there for the first time I sat on a bench and watched the children playing with toys that had come from China. They were all dressed in Chinese costumes. For once, I didn't have a sketch pad with me. It was around Christmas time and the children were practicing the Lion Dance. One little boy looked up and said to me, 'You're the one in the motion pictures. You're a gangster!' And I said, 'No! I'm an artist . . . I just want to make pictures of you kids! I'm coming tomorrow night and I'm going to sketch you!'"

Perhaps the boy had remembered Leo's small part in the gangster film, *Scarlet Street.* Doubtful, but at any rate, the next night, and for many afternoons and weekends afterward, Leo

returned again and again, drawing materials in hand. He would
sit on the bench near the wishing well, his little dog Poupee by
his side. As Leo drew, children peered over his pad and watched
their world take shape on the page. Says Bill Chun-Hoon, the
principal of nearby Castelar School, "Leo was a familiar sight in
Chinatown with his sketch pad, sketching, greeting people . . . a
large crowd of children always gathered around him."

Sometimes Leo gave the children money to buy peanuts so
they could feed Poupee. One day, when images and vague ideas
were forming in Leo's mind but a central character still hadn't been
found, Leo told the children his thoughts. He wanted to make a
book about Chinatown, but he wasn't sure how to proceed. He told
them he was looking for a central character for the book he was
working on. The next day two brothers brought their little sister to
meet him. Leo recalled their pride as they announced, "This is the
character for you!" Leo looked at the little pigtailed girl holding her

Here are a few of the many sketches Leo created for Moy Moy.

big brothers' hands. Moy Moy was tiny, only four years old, and very cute. *Yes*, he thought, *this is the character for me*. The main event, he decided, would be the Chinese New Year, a colorful, action-packed time of year for the Chinese community.

Moy Moy's real name was Mary. "Moy Moy" means "little sister" and was the name her brothers called her. Leo changed her name from Mary to Lily. The name of her street, Chung King Road, became Chanking Street. Until she was ten, Mary and her family lived above her parents' gift shop that is pictured in the story.

Moy Moy and her brothers live on Chanking Street in Los Angeles. There are many brightly colored shops on the street, and one of these belongs to Moy Moy's family. (Moy Moy)

The real Moy Moy and her brothers pose at Robinson's Department Store in downtown Los Angeles. Whenever authors came to the store to sign copies of their new books, they signed them in this room that had been made to look like a library.

Moy Moy and her friends had few real toys. They played jacks or tag, or the dragon game that the children play in the book. All of the children Moy Moy played with lived above their family businesses; it was the only life they knew. Moy Moy and her friends liked to play near the Chinatown wishing well, the spot where Leo would sit and sketch. Moy Moy's school, Castelar Elementary, was only a block away. The family had no car. Everything they needed was in Chinatown.

Moy Moy didn't learn English until she started kindergarten, so she spoke only Chinese when Leo first knew and wrote about her. Her parents didn't speak English at all. She and her brothers went to Chinese school after regular school. They learned Chinese calligraphy, using brushes just as they do in Leo's book.

In the story, there is a huge paper lion that is to star in the parade. Moy Moy is terrified when she first sees it, but a wise older friend suggests that she put her head in the lion's mouth to see that it isn't real. Today, Mary says, "I can't remember if I really did that, but I was fearful of many things as a young child, perhaps even of Leo's little dog. Perhaps my fearfulness gave him the idea for that scene in the story."

Over the course of working on the illustrations for *Moy Moy*, Leo told his editor, "I never had so much fun in my life. At one time I was tired and went to browse around in the shops. Before I left I gave the children a sheet each from my pad and let them use my pencils and watercolors. Soon, from inside the shop, I heard them calling, 'Artist, artist, where are you, artist?'"

Chapter 8
Historic Los Angeles

Leo loved people, especially children, but he also loved buildings. Over time, Leo became more and more interested in the architecture in and around Los Angeles. It grieved him to see the wonderful old houses decaying, then disappearing, to make way for what he called "faceless modern skyscrapers." In an interview with Rosemary Hite, a writer for the *Redlands Sun* newspaper, Leo said, "It would be a sin to lose the old buildings, like losing something valuable in a museum. We must keep our roots alive and functioning or we have nothing."

Years later, when interviewed for an article in another local newspaper, the *Tidings*, Leo spoke about his adopted city. "When I first came to Los Angeles it was a place of magic to me. It was much simpler then, and slower, and the hills circled the basin without buildings and great highways cutting into them." While taking a tour of the new downtown with a writer for the *Downtown News*, Leo chuckled and commented, "I feel like a fly, like a mosquito. Everything is so immense, so glamorous."

Bunker Hill, home of the city's elite from the late 1880s until the 1920s, was Leo and Helen's first home. No longer the posh neighborhood it had once been, the Bunker Hill area was nonetheless where the Politis lived contentedly for many years. Sadly, by the 1950s and 1960s, years after Leo and Helen had moved to Echo Park, the Hill's stately old Victorian homes were destroyed one by one. Roads were erased, and the once beautiful rise of land crisscrossed by winding streets was leveled off.

Leo had written *Rosa* and *Lito the Clown* in the years following the publication of *Moy Moy*, but decided it was time to turn his attention to what was happening to his old, beloved neighborhood. He immortalized what was left of the historic houses the way he knew best: in paint. *Bunker Hill, Los Angeles: Reminiscences of Bygone Days*, published in 1964, was the first book Leo wrote and illustrated for older readers. He spoke for many with this passage:

> There is no doubt that a great number of Angeleños hoped that some of the old homes could have been preserved. Or even that the streets which ran so rhythmically with the contour of the Hill could have remained as they were, and the new built to adjust to the old. By doing so we could have retained some of the city's heritage in this delightful area . . . By destroying all our islands of heritage we are not only erasing the continuity of our city's history, but above all we are denying our children the precious knowledge of the past which would greatly enrich their lives.

In preparing *Bunker Hill*, Leo made a great many sketches, causing Helen much anxiety. Why? Often Leo climbed high up on a house or office building in order to get the right angle for his artwork. Helen was terrified that he would fall and injure himself.

The black-and-white line drawing found inside the covers of this book was drawn by Leo as he stood atop the old Water and Power Building.

When *Bunker Hill* was complete, it not only contained lovely watercolor paintings of the formerly affluent neighborhood, but charming descriptions of the historic old buildings and the people who lived in them. Some thirty years after its publication, Leo recalled with a grin that one such occupant, Miss Nell McKinzie, was less than pleased with Leo's rendering of her home: she didn't like the way he had painted her grass! That critic aside, reading the book is like stepping back into the glory days of the city. And it was a good thing Leo made the book, for the destruction of Bunker Hill continued. Yes, a few of the Victorian houses were scooped up and moved to another part of the city, but Bunker Hill as Leo knew it had vanished. Gone, also, at least for a time, was Angels Flight, the tiny funicular railway that took people from the bottom of Bunker Hill to the top. Then, in the mid-1990s, after nearly thirty years of disuse, Angels Flight was refurbished, and began taking

This painting was used as a poster for *Bunker Hill*, Leo's 1964 tribute to a once-glamorous neighborhood that was forever changed by real estate developers.

customers again. Unfortunately, a fatal accident in 2001 caused the tiny railway to stop making its short, steep journey once and for all. It is only in the pages of *Piccolo's Prank*, Leo's picture book about a curious spider monkey and his adventure on the railway, that the Angels Flight of long ago lives on.

Leo and Helen rented their first Bunker Hill home for close to ten years. After they had been married for nine years, Paul was born there. Now a "family man," Leo had the urge to own his own home, so he moved the family off the hill to nearby Edgeware Road, to a section known as Echo Park. There, in a house south of the Hollywood Freeway, Paul and Suzanne grew up. Leo's next—and last—home was also on Edgeware Road, at the top of the hill, on the north side of the freeway.

It seemed wherever he moved, freeways, big buildings, and other forms of so-called progress were changing Leo's beloved city. Anxious to document the historic parks and traditional festivals before they, too, disappeared, Leo wrote and illustrated *Tales of the Los Angeles Parks* in 1966 and *The Poinsettia* in 1967. In the foreword of *Tales of the Los Angeles Parks*, Leo wrote, "It is imperative that what few patches of wilderness we have left must be preserved." *The Poinsettia* describes various Christmas and Chanukah festivals that light up Los Angeles in winter. You can sense Leo's excitement as he introduces his readers to celebrations that are perhaps unfamiliar to them, beginning with the Legend of the Poinsettia.

Over the next twenty-five years Leo produced two other books created with the older reader in mind. Leo was looking for a way to connect readers young and old to the world around them, a world in danger of slipping away. *Redlands Impressions*, published in 1983, is a tribute to the old mansions of Redlands, California, a town some sixty miles east of Los Angeles. Leo was charmed by the elaborate houses there, Victorian mansions framed by orange groves. "I fell in love with the old structures. Modern houses don't have bad design, but they are not at all interesting to draw." Similarly, modern transportation may be more efficient, but it is seldom as amusing as transportation in the "olden days," particularly if mules were involved. Leo wrote about one such pair of typically uncooperative animals, meant to pull a streetcar up a hill to the town's famous Terracina Hotel. "The first years the car was pulled by a pair of mules. Sometimes the animals got stubborn and refused to go and the passengers helped to push the car up the incline." Leo had wanted to set a picture book in this town he so loved, but it never came to be. "You can't force yourself into a story," he told *Redlands Sun* writer Rosemary Hite. "It has to come spontaneously."

In *Angeleño Heights*, published in 1989, Leo again tells the stories of grand old houses and the people who lived in them. Leo himself lived in Angeleño Heights; his last Edgeware Road home was there. Another hilly area of the city, Angeleño Heights has some houses that look much as the Bunker Hill homes must have looked. Carroll Avenue, in particular, has some beautiful old Victorian homes. Fearing that perhaps they, too, would some day be gone, Leo created pages that lock in the architecture and atmosphere—the very way life felt. Over a dozen charming, one-of-a-kind houses and their residents are profiled in Leo's writing, photos, and, of course, artwork.

The Weller's Mansion was built in the late 1800s at the base of Bunker Hill, and soon after was moved to Angeleño Heights (the area where Leo also moved).

In 1900, Mr. Weller decided to move the mansion . . . to a higher location with a more attractive view overlooking the city to the south and Elysian Hills to the north. It was moved in two sections by a team of horses. He did this while his wife and children were vacationing because he wanted to surprise them on their return.

(They were, as you might imagine, surprised.) (Angeleño Heights)

In order to get a feeling for everyday life in turn-of-the-last-century Los Angeles, Leo interviewed people who had spent their early years in Angeleño Heights. Here's an anecdote about one Morey Holmes. The action takes place around the year 1900, when Morey was nine-years-old.

Morey and his friends took a wide board and put skate wheels on it (each boy had his own). The board was wide enough for them to get on it. They secured ropes on to guide it, and rolled down Carroll Avenue to the end, turned around, and came back again. Mrs. Pinney (the neighbor) went just about crazy from the noise.

Skateboarders, way back then!

With these books, Leo paid homage to a bygone era of California architecture, lifestyle, and community. Leo felt strongly about the need to save historic buildings. He fought for so many preservation causes that he soon became a familiar sight at City Hall.

About two dozen of Politi's Bunker Hill paintings were exhibited at Los Angeles's Bridge Gallery in April 1984. Describing the opening of the exhibit, Jack Smith, *Los Angeles Times* columnist, wrote, "There are real people in Politi's paintings. People he knew, 'Here,' he tells us, 'running around Grandmother's house are Ruby, Julie, Susie, and little Billy; his great big blue eyes were always filled with wonder. These were the last children to live on the Hill. They brought life and joy."

Said one longtime resident:
We children liked to follow the ice wagon. When the horse stopped, we would climb in the back and eat chips. And when we heard the music from the organ-grinder we ran in the house to get our pennies to give to the little monkey.
(Angeleño Heights)

In describing Leo, Jack Smith says, "His hair is gray but thick and wiry. His clothes are on the bohemian side. Has he ever been in a suit? Maybe for his beautiful daughter's wedding? I realized suddenly what it was about him. The older Leo Politi got, the more he looked like one of those houses on Bunker Hill: flamboyant, exuberant, irreverent of style, creaky, slightly out of plumb, and glowing from within through the twilight.

"He was signing my book, elaborately as before. He looked up at me, the wise-owl eyes smiling.

"'Do you want birds?' he asked. I asked for birds."

Chapter 9

Puppets, Parades, and a Four-Year Puzzle

Remember Bill Sousa? He was one of the Olvera Street kids, and one of the inspirations for *Pedro, the Angel of Olvera Street*. As a child, Bill often helped in his older brother Tony's store. Tony sold Mexican folk art, but he also sold Leo's books. Customers often asked whether Leo could sign the books they purchased. Whenever four or five books piled up waiting for signatures, Bill or Tony sent a postcard to Leo and he came to the store. With the same focus he gave to all his creations, Leo turned each signature page into a work of art, not only adding a personal message but also drawing and painting birds, an angel, or a character from the book he was signing. The ink splotches that inevitably dripped from Leo's old-fashioned pen onto the page were incorporated into the piece. Somehow, he never got a drop on himself.

Bill had inspired Leo's art, and perhaps Leo inspired Bill, for he, too, went on to a child-centered career in the arts. In fact, he became a puppeteer, Leo's "other" favorite career choice. Bill had a puppet show called

"Reading Railroad." He and his business part-ner, Bob Schonzler, selected books from various cultures to feature in their show. *Pedro, the Angel of Olvera Street* was one of the plays they performed in schools throughout Los Angeles. It brought Leo's writing to the attention of many principals and teachers who had been unfamiliar with him. One summer, Reading Railroad appeared at a much larger venue than a grade school classroom: the Hollywood Bowl. A well-known outdoor concert hall, the Bowl has featured such famous performers as Leonard Bernstein, Frank Sinatra, the Beatles, and even Big Bird. This particular morning, in a special program just for children, Bill and his partner performed *Pedro*. Leo was in the audience, enjoying every moment. It was all the sweeter that Bill and Bob began by dedicating the show to him. After that, Leo attended their performances whenever he could, wherever they were.

In his sixties—the age that many people begin to consider retiring—Leo's books just kept on coming. During the years 1969 to 1978, Leo produced five more books for children. *Mieko* takes place in Little Tokyo (also known as Japan Town). In it, young Mieko enthusiastically prepares a surprise for her parents, not realizing she is the one who will be surprised. *Emmet*, a dog who nabs babies' toys, chases cats, and is generally never far from trouble, features one of Leo's many real-life dogs. *Three Stalks of Corn* and *The Nicest Gift* focus on Mexican culture and the trea-sures of family life.

Mieko is the only book Leo wrote about Los Angeles's Japanese community. Young and eager, Mieko plans to surprise her parents by becoming queen of the local annual parade. While she does become quite skilled at the traditional dances and other talents required of the queen, there is one important attribute she doesn't have . . . yet. (*Mieko*)

Leo loved his dogs. In *Emmet*, his sixteenth book, about a cat-chasing, mischief-making dog, his own, real-life dogs are the inspiration. The dedication reads: *To Emmet, Poupee, Oscar, Puff, and all the dogs in the world*

The very last book that Leo both wrote and illustrated was *Mr. Fong's Toy Shop*. Published in 1978, *Mr. Fong's Toy Shop* features some of the characters last seen in *Moy Moy*, published eighteen years earlier. Among the repeat characters are the real Mr. Fong, who in *Moy Moy* is shown varnishing a table outside a furniture store.

Have you ever written a story and based the characters on people you know? Perhaps you changed someone's name, hair color, or other characteristics. Authors and artists do that all the time, choosing what they want to use of real people, places, things, and events. They also decide how they want to use them. Although the title is *Mr. Fong's Toy Shop*, at the time the book was written the real Fong's store sold models and miniatures—not toys. The neighborhood children were more likely to be found playing out front than browsing inside. Another trivia twist: the huge kites that hang from the ceiling in Gim Fong's store appear not in *Mr. Fong's Toy Shop* but in *Moy Moy*. Is Gim Fong the Mr. Fong in the book? No. That Mr. Fong was actually based on Gim's picturesque father, who had a long beard and flowing white hair. The elder Mr. Fong had a business in China City, a block away from Olvera Street. In his story, Leo put the elder Mr. Fong in his son's store—you can do that in fiction!

Gim's store was only a few doors away from the business owned by Moy Moy's parents. Gim, now in his seventies, remembers how cute Moy Moy was as a tiny child. He also remembers the little toy bee that she carried, the toy bee featured in Leo's story.

On the day of the festival, children came from everywhere carrying colorful lanterns they had made for the special occasion. (Mr. Fong's Toy Shop)

The action in *Mr. Fong's Toy Shop* takes place during the Moon Festival, an annual fall event. In it, Mr. Fong teaches a group of children how to make shadow puppets. They also learn how the legendary moon goddess Chang-O can be a child's best friend. *Mr. Fong's Toy Shop* is the only one of Leo's books done entirely in black and white, all delicate pen and ink drawings. Without color, as though lit only by the moon, the illustrations help the reader become aware of Leo's skill in drawing.

The swift and lively lion and dragon dancers led the procession. It was a beautiful parade. The children with lanterns looked like a trail of hundreds of fireflies gleaming in the dark. (Mr. Fong's Toy Shop)

Leo's passion to create was also evidenced on a grand scale—murals. The Biscailuz Building, used for many years as the Mexican Consulate, faces the Olvera Street plaza. On its front wall Leo painted a large, colorful mural. In speaking about his approach to murals, Leo told Nelda Stuck, a reporter for the *Redlands Daily Facts*, "Walls make a mural heavy. A wall says 'You've got to do something like me, sturdy, strong, massive.' A mural can't be delicate. You can be sentimental and pretty and delicate to the extreme on paper, but not on a wall." Not only did Leo paint the mural, he also did the tile and glasswork, as well as the carved wooden ornamentation that tops the doorway leading into the building. Leo saw the mural as part of a larger whole, all the pieces of which—the wall, doors, and even the sidewalk—had to be properly integrated.

The Olvera Street mural shows one of Leo's favorite traditions, the Blessing of the Animals. Dedicated by Timothy Cardinal Manning in April 1978, the mural is filled with colorfully dressed people, a priest who blesses the animals, and the wide variety of creatures that participate in the celebration. A cow, wearing a camellia-covered blanket, leads the parade. The central character in Leo's book, *Juanita*, is also in the painting, along with other characters from that book.

Others portrayed in the mural were a familiar sight around Olvera Street. Leo described the violinist as "a thin, handsome old man. He took the part of the grandfather in my story *Pedro, the Angel of Olvera Street.* The baby in the basket on the donkey is a baby I saw in the arms of her mother sitting on a bench across the street."

The blind harp player was also an Olvera Street regular. He died prior to completion of the mural but was immortalized in the painting. Leo's beloved dogs Emmet and Oscar are playing on the wall beneath the stairway at the base of the painting.

Jack Smith, longtime feature writer for the *Los Angeles Times*, was fascinated with the creation of the mural. He visited often over the four years Leo worked on it. In 1978 Mr. Smith wrote, "I never once saw Politi at work. Instead of being painted, the mural seemed to be emerging of its own volition according to some exquisitely slow time scheme, like a picture puzzle whose pieces had been hidden and were being put in place as each was found." When he attended the dedication, Smith described the seventy-year-old Politi as "gaunt, sinewy, grizzled, slightly stooped, but with large eyes that seem always full of wonder."

On the wall of the Biscailuz Building at the entrance to Olvera Street, Leo painted a large mural depicting one of his favorite Olvera Street happenings, the Blessing of the Animals. This parade was also the subject of his book *Juanita*.

Chapter 10
A Secret Dream Comes True

Did you ever have a secret dream, one you wish would come true but figured was about as likely to become reality as meeting your very own fairy godmother? Leo had such a dream, and luckily for him, fairy godparents come in all forms. Little did Leo know that the person who would grant his wish would be more like a "fairy godson," a child he had unknowingly influenced many years earlier.

Richard Alonzo is one of ten children. His family has lived in Los Angeles for four generations. Now one of the Los Angeles Unified School District's eight district superintendents, he first discovered Leo Politi as a third grader when his teacher read *Pedro, the Angel of Olvera Street* to the class. Richard couldn't believe it. He saw something in that book he'd never seen in any other: himself. Of Mexican descent, it was the first time that Richard had come across a book where the children looked like him.

Like many who advance in education, Richard was a teacher before becoming a school superintendent. As a young teacher, he was assigned to a school in Los Angeles's Pico Union, an immigrant area near downtown. Richard's students were primarily Latino and Asian. Knowing the importance of having kids connect to books, he wanted to read stories featuring ethnic groups with which he hoped his class would identify. Richard remembered his own third-grade experience. *Of course*, he thought, *Leo Politi's books. They were the perfect choice for his new class.*

When Richard later went on to become a school principal, the Pico Union community petitioned to bring him back to their locale. A new school was being built and they wanted him to run it. The Superintendent of the Los Angeles Unified School District agreed. The foundation was laid, concrete poured, textbooks purchased, and teachers hired. But what would the school be called? In 1990, a committee was formed to select just the right name. In a move comparable to putting a magic wand into Richard's hands, the school board changed its naming policy: schools could now be named for living people.

After others had had their say and one name after another was eliminated, Richard spoke up. He told the group that no school had been named for a living person who had contributed to children's literacy—an author. Heads nodded in agreement. The committee members were intrigued. They asked him if he had anyone in mind, perhaps someone from his childhood? In no time, Leo Politi became a candidate. He not only lived nearby, he also wrote about the multicultural communities of Los Angeles. It looked as though Leo's fantasy would become reality.

Richard telephoned Leo and asked how he would feel about having a school named after him. Leo was so happy he cried. He told Richard that having a school named for him had always been a secret dream of his. Richard warned him that there was no guarantee it would happen—it was both a committee *and* a school board decision. But when the committee nominated Leo as its final choice, the school board accepted the proposal without any dissent.

Richard went to Leo's house to tell him the good news. It was the first time they had met. When Leo heard that the new school would indeed be named Leo Politi Elementary School, once again his large blue eyes filled with tears. His dream had been fulfilled. After that, Richard and Leo became good friends, and Richard visited Leo at his home many times.

Leo Politi Elementary School opened in August 1991. Leo designed a logo for the school and attended the first teachers' meeting. On November 8, 1991, a few days before his 83rd birthday, Leo, his voice high, cracked, and earnest, spoke at the dedication ceremony:

> I feel honored and proud that this beautiful school was named for me . . . If I can do anything to encourage it to be one of the most beautiful schools in the whole world, I will do it with what little energy I have left. All through my life I worked with children, and when I went to schools I drew pictures for them, not because I wanted them to draw like me. I wanted to create enthusiasm, a love for painting, a love for doing little stories. I wanted to create an enthusiasm for things that are beautiful . . . they don't have to copy me . . . they are great artists themselves. Each child is a miracle, a miracle of life.

> Let this school not be just a building—let it be a place with a soul.

Leo continued to visit the school, his relationship with the staff and students deepening. But the more the school staff became acquainted with Leo, the more concerned they grew. He was very bent and thin. They knew that his wife had been extremely ill for some time and that Leo was caring for her during the day. He was only free to paint at night when she was asleep. At Christmas time the school gave him food baskets. There were always cards, notes, and drawings from the staff and students, as well as nuts and fruit, Leo's favorites from his childhood Christmases in Italy. As Leo grew to be more frail, his school visits became less frequent. Finally, he stopped coming altogether.

Today, Leo remains much revered at the school. Every child "knows" him through his books and beautiful artwork. One of the teachers, Jeannie Winn, takes students to visit some of the local sites described in Leo's books: Little Tokyo, Olvera Street, and Capistrano Mission. The books become quite real for them.

Another teacher, Mike Dreebin, is an avid collector of Leo's books. He currently owns multiple copies of each work, over two hundred copies in all. Many of them were in his fifth-grade class-room; others are in the school library. Although he no longer teaches at the school, he is determined that students know and love the man for whom their school is named. Each classroom bears the name of one of Leo's stories, and Mike has presented the classrooms with copies of the appropriate book.

Leo's friend, Sol Grossman, donated twenty-two original Politi paintings to the school. Leo himself presented the school with a book every time he visited, and Scribner's, the publisher of most of his books, provided the school with handsome glass display cases. They are the first things you see as you enter the library—one of two visual reminders that this is indeed Leo Politi Elementary School. The other is a mural above the entrance to the library.

Carlos Callejo, a muralist originally from El Paso, Texas, was commissioned to paint the mural in 1994. It shows Leo with his arms around a group of children. In the painting, Leo is wearing a jacket that the school staff gave him the Christmas after the school was dedicated to him. Carlos was particularly pleased when he was chosen to do the mural because not only had he grown up in Los Angeles, knowing and loving Leo through his books, as an eight-year-old Carlos was chosen to play the part of Pedro for his school's production of *Pedro, the Angel of Olvera Street.*

In time that very library was named for Richard Alonzo, the "fairy godson" who had made Leo's dream come true. Richard left the school in 1996. He says of his legacy, "If there's anything I want to be remembered for in my life, it's naming the school after Leo Politi."

A legacy, something noteworthy we can point to at the end of our lives and proudly say, "I want to be remembered for that," has many forms. But any legacy—be it naming a school or creating a book—has its roots in one place: an idea. One of the ideas for which we might remember Leo Politi—one of his legacies—was his new way of thinking about children's books.

Some ideas—perhaps a method of painting or writing or investigating science—gain even greater appreciation if we consider their originality in the time in which they were first tried. Take an example from the art world. Even those who are not fans of modern art can appreciate the newness, the very modernity, of what was a dramatically different way of thinking about creativity. For as long as anyone could remember, artists had strived for faithful realism: a cat looked like a cat, a tree like a tree. Innovative artists such as Pablo Picasso—painting fractured, shifting faces and forms—brought significant change not just to the art world, but to the whole world.

The same notion of appreciating new ideas applies to themes in children's books. When Leo began his career, stories set in America took place "in the city" or "in the town" or "on the farm," not within a specific ethnic neighborhood. Leo's decision to set stories in the *barrio* (the Spanish-speaking section of a city, in this case, Los Angeles), or in Chinatown, or in Little Tokyo was, for its time, a significant change. Although "multicultural" is a common word and idea now, it wasn't when Leo first started writing books. And his sprinkling of foreign-language words and phrases throughout his pages, that too was a *concepto nuevo*—a new idea.

Done in the mid 1970s, this sketch was based on an idea Leo had for a book set in Central Los Angeles. The book never made it past the idea stage.

No barrier

From a playground we watch the children play. Some are light others dark — but they are all beautiful. All of them have a live force animating their little bodies. All of them run, play, laugh, and cry, and yet if outwardly they look different, they have within the same emotions of life. Each enjoys living; all will later be in the arms of the mothers who love them, live for them and raise them to be good and kind. If we can only understand this force that makes them live — the same love between mother and child, the same desire that you and I have to live; the love — aspirations — dreams like your mother with you, my mother with me — then no dogmas, no prejudices, no fears can stand barriers between man and man.

Leo Politi

About this handwritten piece, Leo said, "I wrote the passage in 1934 in the gloom days of depression and wars for a local magazine." (Years later it was printed in *Words of Life*, edited by Charles L. Wallis, published by Harper and Row.)

Chapter 11
The Politi Family

Suzanne, Leo, and Paul enjoy themselves on the beach at Monterey. It was especially enjoyable for Leo, as he learned that very day that he had been awarded the Caldecott for *Song of the Swallows*.

Leo had admirers far and wide—and very close to home. His son, Paul, greatly respected his father and his work. He was also impressed by his dad's generous nature. One of Paul's favorite Christmases was when he was seven or eight. Suzanne was around five. Every year after Christmas the department stores in downtown Los Angeles threw away all of the broken toys, or toys that had something missing. One day, Leo arrived home with three very large boxes. He walked or took the bus everywhere he went, and he had somehow managed to bring the boxes home on the bus. To his regret, he'd had to leave behind two additional boxes.

"Once the boxes were emptied my dad set to work to repair the toys," says Paul. "When he was done, he gave the toys away. It seemed as if he supplied the whole neighborhood with skates, dolls, cowboy equipment, and other toys. Dad loved toys, especially the old-style toys that were made with tin. He never learned to like plastic! Whenever Dad had gifts to share with the neighborhood, he put them in a pillowcase and we'd go with him while he played Santa. We'd sing carols and 'Jingle Bells' as we delivered the gifts."

Leo and Paul take a ride.

One Valentine's Day, when Paul was still in elementary school, he wanted to buy some cards to hand out in class. As you might guess, Leo never liked store-bought items, not if it was possible to make the item himself. He volunteered to make Paul the Valentine's Day cards, assuring Paul that he and his classmates would like them. Paul bristled at anything that made him seem different from other kids, so he refused his dad's offer. Like most children, Paul wanted to blend in, not stick out. Blend in? Leo? Maybe Paul hadn't yet learned how his father had pretty much lived in an Indian suit in his own early years.

Even the Politi house was flamboyant. As young children, Paul and Suzanne lived south of the freeway. Later, their home was on a different, more historic part of the street north of the freeway. Leo painted designs on everything from the doorways to the trash cans. He transformed the plain wooden fence into a purplish-pink border covered with blue and green curlicues. At Christmas time, Leo's large, homemade angels sat on the porch. Winter, spring, summer, and fall, the house stood out in the neighborhood like a brightly wrapped present in a sea of brown paper. Paul, who did not take delight in this aspect of his dad's creativity, felt that it looked like the witch's house in *Hansel and Gretel*. As a teenager, Paul found it very embarrassing when his friends came by to visit, but cheerfully made the best of it. "My dad is an artist," he would tell them. "You can't miss it."

Helen understood Leo and loved him just as he was. Over time, she helped Paul and Suzanne understand their dad and the way that his creative spirit made him different. She helped them accept that artists cannot conform to living life the way others do, often saying that they were blessed to have Leo in their lives. Paul and Suzanne accepted Helen's maternal wisdom, but Paul couldn't help wishing for just a little conformity, at least in the house's color scheme. He had to admit, though, the place did have one major advantage: it was the only house around with a pool. Two, actually.

Located on a small lot, 415 East Edgeware Road was long and very narrow. A few steps led up to the front door. Leo loved working with cement, and beside the front door he built a small wading pool. It wasn't deep enough to swim in, but it was a fun place for the children to play in on hot days. At the side of the house Leo added a small round fish pond that was filled with goldfish. Helen, a talented gardener, surrounded the pool and pond with pots of colorful flowers.

When the children had grown too big to enjoy the wading pool and wanted to swim, Leo created another, deeper pool at the back of the house. The backyard was really a sunken patio, but on hot days Leo would fill it with water, creating an instant swimming hole. Nearly three feet in depth and twenty gently curving feet long, it was perfect for underwater swimming. Suzanne and Paul loved floating along on inner tubes in the only pool in the neighborhood.

Paul, Leo, and Suzanne sit at the fish pond at 415 East Edgeware Road, with Skippy, their terrier.

Inside, nearly each room performed double duty, the house being both home and artist workplace. At the top of the steps one entered a living room that also served as a painting studio. Easels were propped against every wall of the room, pages from whatever book Leo was working on displayed on them. Next came a room that during the day was the den and sewing room and at night became Leo and Helen's bedroom. After that came the kitchen, bathroom, and a small laundry area. At the back was another den-by-day and bedroom-by-night.

This room was Paul and Suzanne's. Furniture separated the room in half in an attempt to create private sleeping areas for the two.

Leo puttered about the cheery house and around his community, often visiting the garment district not far from home. The small clothing factories gave Leo leftover remnants of fabric and Helen kept them in the front den, in barrels that Leo painted and labeled. They were always sorted by color or pattern: stripes in one barrel, spotted fabrics in another, red in another. As Leo helped Helen organize her fabrics, so she helped him organize his thoughts, observations, and ideas. One of Suzanne's favorite things to do was looking through the scrapbooks Helen made to help Leo with his art. They included all kinds of things Leo loved—butterflies, sunsets, children—all grouped according to subject.

Leo's many interests were evident around the house. He passionately loved dogs, many of whom appeared in his books and paintings. He was forever bringing home new strays. There were so many that Suzanne and Paul can't even remember their names. The first one they do remember was Skippy, a terrier. Then there was Oscar, a dachshund, and Poupee and Puff, two French poodles. It was Poupee who often joined Leo on his trips to Chinatown. Emmet, a medium-sized shorthaired dog—a bit on the lean side—became the star of his own book. In Leo's paintings and drawings, almost all of the dogs look like Emmet. But it didn't go to Emmet's head. He and all the other dogs were very mellow, with sweet, patient dispositions.

Leo also loved birds; brilliantly colored cockatiels and parakeets were part of the family. One parakeet was usually out of the cage, free to fly around. During the night hours when Leo was painting, the parakeet liked to sit on Leo's easel and keep him company. And if the birds and dogs weren't enough, the children's contribution to the menagerie included two pet guinea pigs.

While working or relaxing, Leo liked listening to country western music on the radio or operetta on an old phonograph. He had a particular fondness for the song *Nature Boy* as performed by singer Nat King Cole, playing it repeatedly on the record player. The lyrics (printed on page 93) do seem to apply to Leo's own life. (As a teenager, Paul himself co-wrote a top ten hit with lyrics that could also be applied to Leo. The song, "Those Oldies but Goodies [Remind Me of You]," shows a sentimental fondness for the past, and the emotional pull of earlier, seemingly simpler times.)

On television Leo enjoyed quite a mix, anything from the news to roller derby, wrestling, old movies, and a special favorite, "Candid Camera." Although no cook himself, Leo included recipes in some of his books as a way of bringing to life whatever culture he was writing about. Helen was the cook, and an excellent one. Ever the sidewalk food fan, Leo ate many small meals while he was out, but he always had room for whatever Helen had prepared for him. She never used any recipes, and today, if Suzanne wants to please her children, she tells them she will make one of Gammy's dishes. The highest compliment that any one of Leo and Helen's seven grandchildren can pay to their

Helen Politi looks very glamorous in this undated photo, probably taken sometime in the 1930s.

76

grandmother's cooking is to say, "I found a place where the food tastes almost as good as Gammy's."

Leo wasn't one to help his children with the drudgery of everyday chores such as homework, but when either of them came up with a creative project, Leo was right there to lend a hand. As a teenager, Suzanne made jewelry. Leo always grew excited at the prospect of assisting her. Not only would he help create designs for her jewelry, he was also known to create needlepoint designs for her friends.

Suzanne inherited a lasting interest in and talent for clothing design from both her parents. After Suzanne married and had children of her own, Helen, a skillful seamstress, made their clothes and quilts. But Leo had to have a part in the creative process. He drew and cut out trucks, ducks, or whatever else came into his head. The shapes were then appliquéd onto the clothes.

Leo had always enjoyed doing wood carvings, and he sparked a wood-carving interest in Suzanne's husband, Larry. Not one to waste what was already available, Leo never bought wood, but rather used odd pieces that he found in people's trash. The size and shape of what he found determined what he carved. Working with Leo, and inspired and guided by him, Larry carved a horse, a bird, and other figures.

Suzanne remembers that as a child, when she and her dad went on outings, he usually took her by herself. She treasured their time together. But family trips were fun, too. Leo had a special fondness for the Union train station, located across from the Olvera Street plaza. Often, during school holidays, the Politis would board the train and travel north to visit their relatives in Fresno. The children had wonderful vacations with Helen's family, who grew grapes on their farm. Since both Leo and Suzanne shared a love of grapes, the two of them would often sneak off together to eat the sun-warmed fruit right off the vine. Another favorite Politi family destination was Monterey, where the children enjoyed spending time running and playing on the beach.

Most days, though, Leo was off somewhere in the city, sketching. But the house didn't sit empty. Thanks to Helen, who cared about everyone and everything, the Politi home was always full of young people who came for her support, guidance, and friendship. Suzanne and Paul always had plenty of unofficial

brothers and sisters, and it wasn't unusual for Suzanne to see her friends being encouraged to talk over a cup of tea. When Suzanne started going to the junior high school dances on Friday nights, Helen worked there as a chaperone. Helen enjoyed these nights so much, she worked there long after Suzanne had left the school.

In the late 1950s and early 1960s, a teenage Paul attended Belmont High School. Even in those days gangs were commonplace in the downtown area of Los Angeles. For years, Leo had sketched in Echo Park, Lincoln Heights, and other local Los Angeles parks. Paul's peers knew his dad only as "the artist." Leo loved drawing the children who followed him, and he had sketched many of them when they were five or six years old. As teenagers, quite a number of these same children became gang members. If any of them bothered or threatened Paul, someone would always say, "It's the artist's son. Leave him alone."

Leo certainly was well known. Unlike so many adults, who zoom from home to office in their cars, speaking to no one, Leo was out and about. He was that unusual Los Angeles bird: a pedestrian. This, in a city renowned for freeway traffic and more than two cars per household. Even the funicular railroad, Angels Flight, was billed as "the shortest railroad in the world." No, if you want to get around Los Angeles, car capital of America, you need . . . a car. But not Leo. He would walk here and there, or if need be, use public transportation. There he'd be on a bus, drawing board and paint box in tow, big eyes taking in everything. To be fair, he had tried driving. But after careening his cousin's car right off the road during his first attempt at driving, Leo handed back the keys and stuck to being a passenger.

That is, until years later, when in 1960 at age 17, his son got behind the wheel. When Paul learned to drive, Leo always accompanied him—even though he had no driver's license himself, and clearly was no expert. Perhaps having a teenager in the driver's seat inspired him to learn to drive—the right way. Whatever the reason, a year or so later, in his early fifties, Leo Politi finally had a driver's license and his first car, a small, brand new Studebaker Lark. Leo owned only three cars over his lifetime. He wouldn't buy one unless he liked the design; he wanted a small car with functional features and eye-pleasing lines. Leo never ordered any extras—no radio, no heater, no air conditioner. If only he'd had the car years earlier. He could have brought home all *five* boxes of broken Christmas toys!

Leo became quite the motorist, traveling great distances to places of interest. Though it had been fifty years since he had worn the Indian suit, Leo was as interested in Native American life as ever. A frequent guest at powwows, he once even drove as far as Oklahoma to attend a Cherokee get-together.

While culture was clearly often at the center of Leo's thoughts, sports, too, had their place. During baseball season, he kept close track of his favorite team. At one time, that team was the Dodgers. As Paul was growing up, Leo often took both Suzanne and Paul to see the team play. Paul was sometimes lucky enough to be bat boy. He had a passion for getting the players' autographs on trading cards, and after a game Leo would wait patiently outside the stadium with Paul so that he could get signatures of the players he admired. Leo was struck by how much the autographs meant to his son, a realization that undoubtedly affected the care he took with signatures for his own fans.

But then baseball disaster struck, at least as far as Leo was concerned. When the Dodgers moved to the newly built Dodger Stadium, they not only ruined his beloved Elysian Park, but also caused the removal of the picturesque houses in Chavez Ravine. From then on, Leo *hated* the Dodgers. He always made a point of listening to Dodger games on the radio—just so that he could hear them *lose*! Quickly regrouping, Leo's new favorite team became—fittingly enough—the Angels.

Another local landmark with a special place in Leo's heart was the Watts Towers. A fantastic creation designed by an elderly Italian man who had no engineering or architectural training, the towers are huge multicolored structures of wire, cement, and scraps of colored tile. In August of 1965, the towers—and people in the neighborhood—were at great risk during the Watts Riots, a nearly weeklong period of rioting and destruction in the poor Los Angeles neighborhood. Leo was deeply saddened for the people in the community, for a while entertaining the notion of giving up art and becoming a teacher there. When the riots finally ended, Leo wanted to go to Watts, to make sure the towers were still standing. Friends warned him against setting foot in the riot-torn area, but he didn't listen. Relieved to see the quirky structures still pointing heavenward—they were some of the very few places untouched by the riots—Leo included a painting of them in his 1967 book, *The Poinsettia*.

Earthquakes, too, are a worrying factor of California life. During the Los Angeles earthquake of February 9, 1971—an earthquake measuring 6.6—Leo became truly unnerved. High-rise buildings swayed, windows shattered, and sixty-five people were killed. Olvera Street was a mess. Stalls collapsed and merchandise was scattered everywhere. Leo was terrified. For many nights after the quake he slept under a heavy wrought-iron and wood table.

Years later, in the early hours one January morning in 1994, another earthquake rocked Los Angeles. Once again Leo's concern was for the Watts Towers rather than his own safety. Suzanne, however, was frantic. Her dad didn't answer his phone and she feared the worst. She had a friend check on him to make sure he was unharmed. (Actually, it was in Paul's area of the city where the earthquake had done the most damage, but Paul, too, was unharmed.)

When disaster struck one of Leo's favorite institutions—the Los Angeles Central Library—it struck hard, and his sadness lingered for weeks. Leo had always impressed upon his children the importance of libraries. He was in awe of the work that librarians did. Once, when standing outside Central Library, he told Paul, "Whatever you want to know in life, you're going to find it there if you look hard enough." When the library burned down on April 29, 1986, Leo felt as though he had lost a beloved friend. Devastated to the point of being unable to work, Leo traveled to an old favorite place, the Monterey Peninsula. Deeply distressed by the fire at his beloved institution, Leo did something of immediate use for another library, the Monterey Public Library: he painted a mural on the wall of their Picture Book Room.

Leo understood that beauty and greatness could be fleeting. He also knew that beauty and greatness were all around us, in even the least expected places. Toward the end of his life, Helen was ill and Leo found it increasingly difficult to care for her, himself, and the house. The grass on the front lawn had grown very tall, and to Paul's eyes, unsightly. He offered to cut it for his dad. Leo said no. Paul offered again. Again Leo turned him down. One day, when the place was just too overgrown for Paul to bear, he absolutely insisted and went out to cut the lawn. Leo was not pleased.

When Paul finished, Leo looked forlornly at his yard. "I asked you not to cut the grass," he said sadly.

Paul tried to comfort him. "But Dad, the grass needed to be cut. The weeds were so high."

Leo said, "But there were these weeds that were so beautiful. They were so decorative. I wanted to sketch them."

Leo's life's work—both at home and in his books—was to make sure the small and large wonders of the world were appreciated. Says Paul, "Dad experienced life, and he wanted to share with people, especially children, things that he thought they might not see for themselves—a flower, a culture, a moment."

Even some weeds.

Concludes Paul, "My father went his own way—in life as well as art."

Chapter 12

If You Could Live Your Life Over Again

As Leo grew older, he cared less and less for the condition of his appearance. His voice was even higher and more cracked, his shoulders increasingly bent. When he spoke, his grammar wasn't always perfect—understandable for someone who grew up speaking two languages—but his underlying message was always clear. He had played many roles in his lifetime: author, artist, historian, husband, father, grandfather, uncle, and friend. His love of children was boundless. And everyone, regardless of age and relationship to Leo, was, to Leo, his friend.

In 1989, Leo, 81 years old, was the guest of honor at a celebration held by FOCAL (Friends of Children and Literature). The mayor of Los Angeles, Tom Bradley, delayed at a previous engagement, phoned to apologize for not being present. Leo's longtime friend Sandy Schuckett took the call, then handed the phone to him. "Leo smiled and nodded and made quiet comments on what the mayor was saying to him. When he got off the phone, Leo said softly, 'That was the mayor!'" Sandy smiled, knowing her friend could never quite believe that the mayor thought that he, Leo, was important. "There was a part of Leo that never knew his worth," says Sandy.

His last published work, *Lorenzo the Naughty Parrot*, appeared in 1992. Written by a southern California author, Tony Johnston, the work was illustrated by Leo. It was a story after Leo's own heart, providing him with one last opportunity to share paintings of quaint East Los Angeles houses, old cars, dogs, parrots, and children. As is often the case in children's publishing, author and illustrator did not know each other. But Tony did know of Leo; she had grown up loving him through his books. So it was a special treat when they did meet, at a book signing in Burbank, California. Tony finally met the man she had admired for many years.

A short time before Leo died, his nephew, Norman Niccoll, Marie Therese's son, paid him a visit. Leo gazed at Norman and then said, "I haven't been a very good uncle, have I?" Norman put his uncle at ease. "You've given your love to your art—lived for art's sake. That was far more important than the everyday things in life."

When people asked Leo if there was one book of his that was his favorite, he always said no. But he would go on to explain that he was least satisfied with the ones he worked on for the shortest amount of time. If he happened to be signing one of those to a fan, he would paint a particularly elaborate picture on the first page to make sure that he was giving the recipient something special.

In the last few years of his life Leo remained very independent. He always wanted to handle everything for himself and would discourage anyone else from helping him. Although he continued to work on several book manuscripts, Leo's arthritis became so bad that some days he could only work for thirty minutes at a stretch.

It was a worrying time for Paul and Suzanne. Leo was living alone by this time. He had cared for Helen as long as he could, but she was suffering from Alzheimer's disease and needed to be in a care facility. Though Leo was very frail and needed a walker in order to move around safely, he was still as clear thinking as ever. He refused to live with either of his children. Paul said he would only allow his father to continue living alone if they talked on the telephone every day. Leo agreed but often wouldn't answer his phone.

Paul's office was close by, but Suzanne still had children at home and lived a two-hour journey away. It was much harder for her to help out, but it didn't stop her from worrying.

Just before Leo died, Paul and his wife, Bonnie, took Leo out for a meal. Leo had told Paul that as a child he wanted to be a puppeteer, so Paul asked him, "If you could live your life over again, what would you do differently?"

Leo replied, "I wouldn't change one moment. I think I've had such a blessed life. Every day I just got up and painted."

Helen had always understood that. She pinched pennies to make it possible. Leo never felt pressured to work a regular, nine-to-five job. Later, Paul realized that his dad had spent his life associated with teachers and librarians—people who were dedicated to their professions out of love, not financial gain. And of course, Leo's days were filled with children. Always and foremost came the children.

On February 24, 1996, a month before his death, Leo attended a ceremony celebrating the reopening of Angels Flight, the funicular railway that had been removed from his beloved Bunker Hill many years earlier. Leo cut the ribbon and was the very first passenger to ride on the new railway. It was an exciting day for him. Leo happily signed posters made from his original Angels Flight painting. "My father tried to keep the true spirit of Los Angeles alive," said Paul. "Los Angeles and its history never lost its fascination for him."

This church is in Central Los Angeles, where Leo often went to sketch children at play. Leo created this piece sometime in the 1970s.

Chapter 13
Remembering Leo

Leo Politi died on March 26, 1996. He was 87. On April 8, 1996, letters appeared in the *Los Angeles Times*. Kathleen Turgeon wrote of her experience whenever Leo signed a book for her. "His message would always be a mini work of art, often done with India ink and old steel nib points that were prone to drip on the page. He readily turned the blobs into posies or other decorations that always embellished his letters. On one occasion, when I commented on the ease with which he drew, Leo said simply, 'It's because I do it every day'—a truly humble man."

In another letter, Harvey D. Kern wrote, "Los Angeles has lost a part of its very soul." He added, Leo "has truly earned his place in heaven, and will likely enhance it with portraits of happy young faces reflecting his contributions to countless children (and adults) for nearly 60 years."

It seemed only fitting that a Leo Politi memorial service be held on Olvera Street, close to his Blessing of the Animals mural. The announcement informing the public of the event said that it was "open to all who appreciated the man and his work."

Since Leo hated all talk of death and funerals, there had been no funeral service. His body was cremated. The family obtained permission to bury some of Leo's ashes at Olvera Street. They arrived at the memorial event early and buried the ashes around the base of the olive tree that had been dedicated to him. Later, Leo's ashes were also scattered in every spot that he loved, among them Chinatown, Paul and Suzanne's gardens, and Elysian Park.

On the day of the memorial service, April 22, 1996, hundreds of people gathered to remember Leo Politi. Thom Davis, a longtime friend of the family, served as master of ceremonies. He welcomed the guests with a prayer, then introduced a number of speakers, all of whom had known, admired, and loved Leo.

Inside the memorial program was a piece written by Thom. He said of Leo that his art

> . . . reflects a man who cared about the world and the quality of the environment around him, with a special passion for the City of the Angels. Leo was a simple, humble man who only wanted people to enjoy his art . . . it was the children who melted his heart and inspired him to reach new heights . . . Leo's work captured not only the beauty in life but also the innocence found in life. His love for all children and animals became very apparent in his art and books.

Catherine Siracusa, Leo's younger cousin, was born in 1947, just as Leo's career was taking off. Her childhood home was filled with his books and paintings. Speaking at Leo's memorial, Catherine told those gathered how important his work had been to her:

> When I went to elementary school in California, there were very few Italian children. No one ever knew how to spell my name. But

Leo's books like *Little Leo* and *A Boat for Peppe* talked about Italian children, and made me feel proud of my background . . . His books tell children that coming from a different background makes you special and unique, and that's something to be proud of. Even though I'm sad today, I'm very proud to be Leo Politi's cousin.

Catherine herself went on to become a children's book author and illustrator. Dedicating one of her books to Leo was bittersweet. Although she was pleased to make the tribute, he never saw it. Her book, *The Peanut Butter Gang*, came out one month after his death. As it happens, another book was also dedicated to Leo that year. In *Angels Flight: A History of Bunker Hill's Incline Railway*, author Virginia L. Comer wrote:

To Leo Politi, artist and author, whose graceful art has preserved historic scenes of Angels Flight and Bunker Hill and imbued them with the richness of his own spirit, this book is dedicated with esteem.

When Leo had sketched in Chinatown, he often visited the Castelar Elementary School there. The students and staff loved Leo, and when Dr. Bill Chun-Hoon became principal of the school in 1973, he and Leo became friends. Leo often visited Bill's home, sharing a meal with his family or sketching Bill's daughter.

Bill's words at the memorial reflected not only his feelings, but those of many who admired Leo's work:

We'll always remember Leo Politi walking throughout this historic area of El Pueblo that he loved so dearly, and in Chinatown, just a few blocks away, he was a familiar sight. Leo set two of his stories in Chinatown, *Moy Moy* and *Mr. Fong's Toy Shop*. Both are true representations of Leo's love of family, cultural diversity, and values. Mary Yan Joe, the real Moy Moy, and her family are here today, as well as Gim Fong of *Mr. Fong's Toy Shop*.

At the entrance to Castelar School there is a mural painted by Leo Politi in 1977. It depicts life as seen through his eyes—happy children of various ethnic groups, holding hands and dancing together in a natural setting. This is symbolic of Leo's hope for harmony among people and with nature. That is Leo's trademark.

To all of us, Leo was unassuming, modest, and unpretentious. He didn't like a lot of hoopla or someone making a fuss over him. A poem in his book *Mieko* about a family in Little Tokyo may be characteristic of his life. It reads:

Very soon I shall be gone –
I am just a morning glory,
A fading flower at dawn.

We all know, and I think Leo also knew this, that in his paintings, books, and his personal outlook on life, he left a legacy and a powerful message that will remain with us forever, and that is the basic goodness of people, kindness, love, and respect for others. In these troubled times we need to practice the values that Leo Politi stood for and portrayed so well in his works.

Castelar Elementary School in Chinatown was a favorite of Leo's. He painted this mural for the school.

For many of the people who attended the memorial, most vivid were the memories of times when Leo had autographed a book for them. He always took the time to include an exquisite watercolor painting, a message, and his scratchy, flamboyant signature. All those hours spent outside Dodger Stadium years earlier, patiently waiting as his young son gathered signatures from his favorite players, undoubtedly had had an affect on Leo. "He knew how much those autographs meant to me," says Paul. "He realized that those little signatures meant a lot to people." And not just young fans, either. Both Jackie Kennedy and Ladybird Johnson had sought Leo's special signature, too.

In describing the many hours Leo spent signing books, Leo's friend Sol Grossman said, "Leo always did his finest, whether it was a piece going to press or a book for a nine-year-old."

In 1984, *Los Angeles Times* columnist Jack Smith wrote, "Politi is the world's slowest autographer. I once saw him signing books in a bookstore, and although the line was long, he took his time, making each autograph a work of art."

Leo poses with two of his young friends from Castelar Elementary School.

Created for the author of this book, the nameplate shown here is one of the many personalized inscriptions that Leo did for his fans and friends at the front of his books. Leo would work any ink splotches that dripped from his old-fashioned pen into the art.

*   *   *

Leo's books educate and entertain. His words have beauty. The illustrations are charming as well as skillful. In writing about the people and cultures of Los Angeles, Leo was far ahead of his time, an innovator. It would be years before any other author attempted to write stories that focused on children of other cultures. Leo had a unique talent for creating a strong story that wove history, legends, songs, foods, recipes, customs, and foreign words into a harmonious whole. His contribution to children's literature, and the legacy left by his stories, is immeasurable.

Sadly, there is a melancholy postscript. Of all the books Leo both wrote and illustrated, only one, *Song of the Swallows*, is still in print. Thank goodness for the libraries Leo so cherished. Now they—the final keepers of most of his books—are giving something back to him.

Nature Boy

There was a boy
A very strange enchanted boy;
They say he wandered very far, very far
Over land and sea.
A little shy
And sad of eye,
But very wise was he.
And then one day,
One summer day,
He passed my way.
And we spoke of many things,
Fools and kings,
This he said to me:
The greatest thing you'll ever learn
Is just to love
And be loved in return."

- Eden Ahbez

If you work at it, there is no limit to what you can accomplish, and to the happiness the work of creation can bring to you.

- Leo Politi

Afterword: Some Personal Memories from the Author

I met Leo many times over the last twenty years of his life. Often I watched from a distance as he sketched one of the children playing in the plaza of Olvera Street. He rarely sat down to draw. Standing, he bent over a large drawing board, sheets of sketching paper clipped to it. As his pencil raced across the paper, Leo seemed unaware of the activity buzzing around him in the plaza. His concentration was intense; his face serious. In no time at all Leo would have completed an exquisite drawing.

Whenever I had money to spend, I wrote to Leo and made an appointment to meet him at Philippe's Restaurant, located between Olvera Street and Chinatown. First, we'd eat our evening meal, Leo always choosing beef stew rather than the specialty of the restaurant, French dip sandwiches. Then he'd take me out to his car. There, from the display he set up on the car's trunk, I'd add to my collection of original artwork, or purchase more of his books.

On returning to the restaurant, out would come a small paint box. Leo would painstakingly draw, and then paint, a picture in the front of the book I was purchasing. And always he wrote, "To my friend Ann, with appreciation, Leo." He wrote that from the first time I met him. A crowd would gather to watch him work. The white-coated bus boys were always an attentive audience.

Children motivated Leo in his painting, writing, and drawing. In the last years of his life he was working on a collection of drawings of children for a book that, sadly, never came to be. I loved the drawings and told him so. He shrugged and said, "This was for my book on the children of Los Angeles." But once you had admired a drawing, he insisted on selling it to you, immediately lowering the asking price if he thought you couldn't afford it. He was so appreciative of people who liked his work.

Although I was only one of a great many who Leo addressed as "friend," his death left a hole in my life. Leo was a kind man. A gentle man. His talent can neither be forgotten nor underestimated. It is hard to believe that I will never again sit with him over a bowl of stew, watch him create art, or see his face light up at the approach of a child.

Leo's last drawing to the author, done in 1995. They never saw each other again.

ime Line of Important Events in Leo Politi's Life

1908	Leo Politi born in Fresno, California, on November 21
1914	The Politi family leaves Fresno and moves to Italy. Leo is 6 years old.
1920	Leo and his family spend a year in London; Leo is 12 years old.
1922 to 1928	From age 14 to 20, Leo attends art school in Monza, near the city of Milan. During this period, he spends some months in the army.
1928 to 1930	Leo works as a fabric designer and textbook illustrator.
1930	Leo returns to California by freighter. The boat travels through the Panama Canal and stops in many Central American ports. Leo visits different towns and cities in California before deciding to live in Los Angeles.
1933	Leo settles on Bunker Hill, Los Angeles.
1934	Helen and Leo are married.
1943	Son Paul is born on July 31.
1946	Daughter Suzanne is born on August 22.
1947	*Pedro, the Angel of Olvera Street* is a Caldecott Honor Book.
1949	*Juanita* is a Caldecott Honor Book.
1950	*Song of the Swallows* is the Caldecott Medal Winner.
1961	*Moy Moy* is recognized by the Southern California Council on Literature for Children and Young People for Leo's "significant contribution in the field of illustration."
1966	Leo is awarded the Regina Medal by the Catholic Library Association for his "continued distinguished contribution to children's literature."
1974	A new branch of the Fresno County Public Library is named the *Leo Politi Branch Library*.

1980	FOCAL (Friends of Children and Literature) presents Leo with its very first award, one created for children's book authors working with California themes.
1984	Los Angeles Mayor Tom Bradley declares April "Leo Politi Appreciation Month." On Olvera Street, an olive tree and a ceramic plaque honoring Leo are placed near his Blessing of the Animals mural.
1991	The Leo Politi Elementary School is dedicated.
1994	Monticillo de Leo Politi, an area of Elysian Park, Los Angeles (close to Dodger Stadium), is dedicated to Leo Politi.
1996	February 24, Angels Flight reopens. Leo signs posters and is the first passenger to ride on the new funicular.
	Leo dies on March 26, age 87.
	April 22, a memorial service is held at Olvera Street in Leo's memory.
1997	August 1 to September 1, Olvera Street Retrospective. On display are books, paintings, and wood sculptures representing over 60 years of work.
1999	FOCAL honors Leo posthumously with a program at the Los Angeles Central Library: *Leo Politi's Los Angeles, A Celebration of His Life and Work.*
2001	Helen dies on November 16, age 93.
2004	An illustration by Leo Politi appears in the book *Oscar Night: 75 Years of Hollywood Parties From the Editors of Vanity Fair* by Graydon Carter and David Friend. Afterword by Dominick Dunne, published by Alfred A. Knopf, October 2004.

And finally, Leo and Helen leave behind seven grandchildren:
Michael Paul Politi (February 22, 1966), Martin Kennedy Politi (August 25, 1967), Mitchel Leo Politi (July 17, 1969), Joshua Bischof (June 17, 1977), Matthew Paul Bischof (January 16, 1980), Noah Lawrence Bischof (September 3, 1984), and Harmony Suzanne Bischof (September 16, 1987)

Books for Children Written and Illustrated by Leo Politi

1938	*Little Pancho*, Viking Press
1946	*Pedro, the Angel of Olvera Street*, Charles Scribner's Sons
1947	*Young Giotto*, The Horn Book
1948	*Juanita*, Charles Scribner's Sons
1949	*Song of the Swallows*, Charles Scribner's Sons
1950	*A Boat for Peppe*, Charles Scribner's Sons
1951	*Little Leo*, Charles Scribner's Sons
1953	*The Mission Bell*, Charles Scribner's Sons
1957	*The Butterflies Come*, Charles Scribner's Sons
1959	*Saint Francis and the Animals*, Charles Scribner's Sons
1960	*Moy Moy*, Charles Scribner's Sons
1963	*Rosa*, Charles Scribner's Sons
1963	*Lito and the Clown*, Charles Scribner's Sons
1965	*Piccolo's Prank*, Charles Scribner's Sons
1967	*The Poinsettia*, Best-West
1969	*Mieko*, Golden Gate Junior Books
1971	*Emmet*, Charles Scribner's Sons
1973	*The Nicest Gift*, Charles Scribner's Sons
1976	*Three Stalks of Corn*, Charles Scribner's Sons
1978	*Mr. Fong's Toy Shop*, Charles Scribner's Sons

Books for Children and Adults, Written and Illustrated by Leo Politi

1964   *Bunker Hill, Los Angeles*, Desert Southwest
1966   *Tales of the Los Angeles Parks*, Best-West
1983   *Redlands Impressions*, Moore Historical Foundation
1989   *Angeleño Heights*, self-published by Leo Politi

Books Illustrated for Other Authors

1941   *The Least One* by Ruth Sawyer, Viking Press
1942   *Aqui se Habla Español* by Margarita Lopez, D. C. Heath and Co.
1944   *Angelo the Naughty One* by Helen Garrett, Viking Press
1944   *Stories from the Americas* by Frank Henius, Charles Scribner's Sons
1946   *The Three Miracles* by Catherine Blanton, John Day Co.
1947   *El Coyote the Rebel* by Luis Perez, Henry Holt and Co.
1949   *At the Palace Gates* by Helen Rand Parish, Viking Press
1949   *Vamos a Hablar Español* by Margarita Mesas and Esther Brown, D. C. Heath and Co.
1950   *Magic Money* by Ann Nolan Clark, Viking Press
1952   *Looking-for-Something* by Ann Nolan Clark, Viking Press
1955   *The Columbus Story* by Alice Dalgliesh, Charles Scribner's Sons
1957   *Building Our Hemisphere* by Clyde B. Marks, Charles Scribner's Sons
1961   *Magic Doll* by Elizabeth Coatsworth, Viking Press
1962   *All Things Bright and Beautiful* by Cecil Frances Alexander, Charles Scribner's Sons
1984   *Two Girls and a Kite* by Edith Parker, Moore Historical Foundation
1986   *Around the World, Around our Town*, Friends of San Pedro Library
1992   *Lorenzo the Naughty Parrot* by Tony Johnston, Harcourt Brace Jovanovich

Subject Guide to Children's Books
Written and/or Illustrated by Leo Politi

Little Pancho
1938

The jungle, Central America
A young boy wanders off into the jungle after his mother has told him to stay home.

Pedro, the Angel of Olvera Street
1946

Olvera Street, Los Angeles
Christmas, Mexican traditions, Las Posadas, piñatas

Young Giotto
1947

Italy
The story of Saint Francis, this book was a fifty-cent insert in *The Horn Book* Christmas issue.

Juanita
1948

Olvera Street, Los Angeles
Easter, Blessing of the Animals, Mexican Americans, Catholic religious traditions

Song of the Swallows
1949

San Juan Capistrano, California
Swallow migration, California Missions, Father Junipero Serra, Saint Joseph's Day

A Boat for Peppe
1950

Monterey, California
Fishing village, Italian Americans, Festival of Saint Rosalia

Little Leo
1951

Fresno, California and San Matteo, Italy
Italian Americans, immigration

The Mission Bell
1953

El Camino Real, California
Founding of the California Missions, Father Junipero Serra, Chumash Indians

The Butterflies Come 1957	*Monterey Peninsula, California* Monarch butterflies, migration, metamorphosis, Chumash Indians, butterfly festival
Saint Francis and the Animals 1959	*Assisi, Italy* Saint Francis, Italian village life, animals
Moy Moy 1960	*Chinatown, Los Angeles* Chinese Americans, Chinese New Year, lion and dragon parades, Chinese language and writing
All Things Bright and Beautiful 1962	Old English hymn by Cecil Frances Alexander
Rosa 1963	*San Felipe, Baja California* Mexico, village life, deserts, Christmas in Mexico, piñatas
Lito and the Clown 1963	*Mexico* Village life, clowns, traveling circus
Piccolo's Prank 1965	*Bunker Hill area of Los Angeles* Angels Flight cable car, organ-grinders and monkeys, Victorian houses
The Poinsettia 1967	*Los Angeles, California* Christmas and Chanukah traditions
Mieko 1969	*Little Tokyo, Los Angeles* Japanese Americans, Nisei Week, Ondo parade
Emmet 1971	*Los Angeles* A brave dog saves a grocery store from burning down.
The Nicest Gift 1973	*East Los Angeles* Mexican Americans, El Mercado, Christmas
Three Stalks of Corn 1976	*East Los Angeles* Mexican Americans, importance of corn, Mexican foods, Mexican legends
Mr. Fong's Toy Shop 1978	*Chinatown, Los Angeles* Chinese Americans, Moon Festival, moon goddess Chang-O, shadow puppets
Lorenzo, the Naughty Parrot 1992	*Mexico* Piñatas, village life, Christmas, brick making

List of Illustrations